Antiques at a Glance

GLASS

Antiques at a Glance

GLASS

JAMES MACKAY

PRC

First published 2002 by
PRC Publishing Ltd,
64 Brewery Road, London N7 9NT

A member of **Chrysalis** Books plc

This edition published 2002
Distributed in the U.S. and Canada by:
Sterling Publishing Co., Inc.
387 Park Avenue South
New York, NY 10016

© 2002 PRC Publishing Ltd

ISBN 1 85648 628 1

Printed and bound in China

All the images were kindly supplied by © Christie's
Images Ltd 2002.

Contents

Introduction
The History of Glass

Humanity is perhaps not unique in the habit of storing up objects for their own sake, but is the only animal capable of translating material possessions into other values and assessing their worth in terms of hard cash.

According to *The Encyclopaedia Britannica* "antique" means "old" but also carries connotations of esthetic, historic, or financial value. Formerly the term was applied to the remains of the classical cultures of Greece and Rome, now more specifically labeled as "antiquities," but gradually "decorative arts, courtly, bourgeois and peasant, of all past eras" came to be considered antique.

This definition is somewhat vague, though it hints that mere age alone is not sufficient to make an object worthy of the appellation "antique." *The Oxford English Dictionary* is even more vague in its definition: "Having existed since olden times; of a good age, venerable, old-fashioned, antiquated such as is no longer extant; out of date, behind the times, stale; of, belonging to, or after the manner of any ancient time; a relic of ancient art, of bygone days."

The legal definition of an antique also varied considerably from one country to another. The United Kingdom Customs and Excise Tariff Act of 1930 specified that objects manufactured before 1830 (i.e. a hundred years old or more) would be regarded as antique and therefore exempt from payment of duty on import. The United States Tariff Act of 1930 exempted from duty "Artistic antiquities, collections in illustration of the progress of the arts, objects of art of educational value or ornamental character... which shall have been produced prior to the year 1830." Across the border in Canada, however, their Customs Tariff Act of 1948 defined as antiquities "all objects of educational value and museum interest, if produced prior to 1st January 1847."

Legal definitions, originally designed to cover material a century old, became fixed in such a way as to exclude anything produced after the Regency period. It was often stated that the main reason for adhering to the year 1830 was the fact that craftsmanship deteriorated after that date. For this reason bodies, such as the British Antique Dealers' Association, clung to 1830 as the chronological criterion in defining an antique.

As time passed, however, this inflexible ruling seemed more and more untenable from a purely legal viewpoint, and for the purpose of the avoidance of the payment of import duty the date criterion was subsequently modified in certain countries. The United Kingdom Customs and Excise Tariff Act of 1959, for example, outlined that duty would not be payable on the import of objects, "if manufactured or produced as a whole, and in the form as imported, more than a hundred years before the date of import." More recently, the United States customs adopted a straightforward hundred-year rule, and with the advent of Value Added Tax and similar imposts in other countries, the hundred-year rule is now widely observed.

In periods of economic uncertainty interest in collectable objects tends to increase at the expense of

more traditional forms of investment. What used to be the principal motive in collecting—a need to identify with the past—has tended to yield to a need for the form of security that the possession of tangible objects brings when money itself is diminishing in worth and true meaning. It becomes less important to the collector to amass objects of great antiquity, especially since the supply of antiques has become scarcer due to worldwide demand, and leads the collector to turn inevitably to more recent products. For those reasons, many dealers in the 1970s and 1980s adopted a fifty-year rule, so that objects of the 1920s and 1930s could be encompassed. First the artifacts of the late-Victorian and Art Nouveau periods became perfectly acceptable, and were then rapidly followed by Art Deco and the products of the immediate prewar period. Now date lines have been virtually abandoned as collectors and dealers discover newer and newer objects on which to focus their attention.

Greater flexibility in defining what might be regarded as an antique came not a moment too soon, as the supply of fine-quality pieces produced before 1830 had all but dried up by the 1960s. At the same time, many museums with seemingly unlimited funds were intent on expanding their collections. This meant that the amount of quality antiques available to the market began to dry up, as well as having the unfortunate effect of pushing up the market value of what material was left. Some categories of antiques, such as 16th and 17th century silver, early Meissen and Chelsea porcelain, and Ravenscroft glass, soon went beyond the reach of all but the wealthiest collectors. Not only did museums tend to create a shortage of material

LEFT: A Wiener Werkstätte light, the design attributed to Koloman Moser.

available to the private collector but, by imaginative and intelligent use of their acquisitions, they heightened the interest of established collectors and laymen alike, thereby increasing the demand for antiques still further.

While this tendency was gathering momentum in the 1960s and 1970s, the growing interest in the private sector was inevitable anyway. A higher level of general prosperity and higher standards of education were only two of the factors that made the public not only more appreciative of all that was best from times past, but also gave them the money to indulge their tastes. Traditionally antique collecting had been the closed preserve of the upper classes, who had the money, the education, and the social background to indulge their tastes. Collecting antiquities developed in Renaissance Italy and spread slowly to more northerly countries. In Britain, for example, the fashion for collecting things of the past only really began to develop in the late 18th century. Emphasis was laid on classical antiquities, fostered by the classical education of the times as well as the acquisitive habits picked up during the obligatory Grand Tour.

From then on, an antiquarian interest in the material objects of the past tended to lag behind by one or two centuries. Collectors of the Regency era discovered an interest in Tudor and Jacobean furniture, the Victorians looked to the Restoration and early Georgian period, and the Edwardians had the highest regard for the products of the 18th and early 19th centuries. In general, collectors and cognoscenti alike disregarded the products of their immediate forebears, which explains why the 1830 rule endured as long as it did.

Interest in collectables has also gone in cycles. There are five or ten year highs and lows in different categories, as well as periods of slump due to socio-political and economic factors. Antiques that came on to the market in 1917 or 1942, for example, could be picked up for a song. However, people didn't have the money to spend in those years, and there was a general reluctance to invest in material that might be destroyed by enemy action or plundered in the uncertainties of war.

Conversely, the economic upheavals of the late 1960s and early 1970s led to a flight of money out of traditional forms of investment, such as stocks, shares, unit trusts, real estate, and building societies, and into art and antiques. The devaluation of sterling in November 1967 and the subsequent run on the dollar and then the franc created a wave of near hysteria in the antique markets of Europe and America. The leading salerooms reported a 50 percent increase in turnover in the ensuing 12 months alone, right across the board, although in certain categories the turnover was up by as much as 100 percent (for prints and drawings), while silver sales increased by 69 percent.

Coupled with this astonishing increase in sales, it was significant that the leading salerooms on both sides of the Atlantic began diversifying into material of more recent vintage than was generally accepted as antique, and this trend has steadily developed ever since. This even led to the development of separate auction houses, such as Christie's in South Kensington, London, catering specifically to the "newer" antiques, including many articles that would not have been regarded as collectable a few years previously.

The major salerooms, as well as the multitudes of lesser auction houses, were only encouraging a trend that was already there. In the same way, the junk shop of yesteryear has been elevated to the antique shop of today; the weekend junk stall or barrow in a street market has become a booth in a permanent antique market; and the better pieces traded in markets rapidly move up the scale, with a corresponding mark-up in price at each stage.

As the amount of quality antiques available to the market dwindled, it seemed paradoxical that antique shops were proliferating everywhere at an astonishing rate. The number of good antique shops remained fairly static, nor did they find it any easier to obtain quality material for their stock. The answer to this paradox was, at first, a general lowering of standards; if you clung to increasingly untenable date lines, whether 1830 or 1870, then it was inevitable that you had to settle for second-best or some sacrifice in workmanship, condition, or quality.

The more astute collectors ignored date lines and explored the potential of later material. If the products of the Baroque, Rococo, and Neo-classical periods were no longer available, might not there be much to commend in, say, the products of the Second Empire in France, the Biedermeier era in Germany, or the Victorian era in general?

It was fashionable at one time to write off the entire Victorian period as one of uniformly bad taste. Much of the opprobrium heaped on the bourgeois fashions of the 19th century by subsequent generations was undeserved. It is true that in furniture and art, as in the material comforts of everyday life, the Victorians showed a predilection for the massive, the ornate, and the fussy; but not all was tawdry or tasteless by any means.

That the Victorians were capable of perpetrating, and apparently enjoying, objects of unbelievable hideousness is true, but at the same time there were serious attempts to raise standards. The much-abused Great Exhibition of 1851 did more than is often realized to encourage pride in craftsmanship and demonstrate that a thing could be beautiful as well as functional. Though much that is Victorian was, not so long ago, regarded as hardly worth preserving, there were many other things that possessed enduring qualities, and were recognized as such by discerning collectors, long before such objects had earned the title or dignity of antique. It has to be added that even the fussy and the florid, the over-ornamented and the downright ugly from that much-maligned period have acquired a certain period charm. Truly, distance does lend enchantment.

Conscious efforts to improve public taste and foster pride in workmanship seem like oases in the wilderness of materialism and mass production. In England, the Arts and Crafts Movement inspired by William Morris in the 1880s was an attempt to recapture something of the primeval simplicity in craftsmanship—a reaction against the pomposity and over-ornateness of Victorian taste. It was a precursor of that curious phenomenon at the turn of the century known as Art Nouveau in Britain, as *Jugendstil* ("youth style") in Germany, or as Liberty style in Italy (from the well-known London department store which was one of its great proponents).

The practitioners of the New Art went back to nature for inspiration, and invested their furniture, glass, silver, and ceramics with sinuous lines and an ethereal quality. In turn, this provoked a reaction that resulted in the straight lines of the Bauhaus and the geometric forms associated with Art Deco in the inter-war period. It has to be admitted that these styles and fashions seemed ludicrous to many people at the time, especially in their more exaggerated forms; nevertheless they were the outward expression of a minority in art, in architecture, in furniture, textile, and ceramic design, which strove for improvements (as they saw it) in the production and appearance of objects. These were not only objects

intended purely for decorative purposes, but those used in every phase and aspect of life.

The products of the Arts and Crafts Movement, of Art Nouveau and Art Deco were despised and neglected in succession, and then, after a decent lapse of time, people began to see them in their proper perspective and appreciate that they had a great deal to offer to the collector.

Nevertheless, it is also fair to comment that the century after 1830 was a barren one as far as the production of fine-quality material was concerned. Thirty years ago collectors made a fine distinction between what was merely old but had no particular merit on grounds of esthetic features or workmanship, and those objects which had some qualities to commend them. Nowadays, however, as demand continues to outstrip supply, there is a tendency to talk up wares that may be old, but are commonplace and mediocre nonetheless. The insatiable demand especially at the lowest end of the market decrees that this should be so, but it is important for the collector to discriminate and learn to recognize the features and factors that distinguish the worthwhile from the second-rate. Ultimately these are the factors that govern the soundness of any investment in antiques.

In the course of this century there have been startling developments in education, communications, travel, and living standards. People are generally more affluent today than were their parents or grandparents. They enjoy shorter working hours and a larger surplus disposable income. Through education and such external stimuli as the cinema and also television

LEFT: A selection of engraved Bohemian goblets dating from around 1900.

programs, a lot more people have a greater awareness of things of beauty or of antiquarian interest. More and more people now have the time and the money to indulge in collecting objects, which in the past was the preserve of a privileged few.

A greater general awareness of what is beautiful and worthwhile inevitably tends to encourage better craftsmanship. Despite the general perception of the period between the two world wars as the nadir in fine design and workmanship, there were also many individuals and groups who were active in Europe and America in promoting design consciousness. Today, the products of their studios and workshops, especially in the fields of furniture, ceramics, glass, and metalwork, are deservedly sought after and fetch correspondingly high prices. This trend has continued to the present day, with the result that each year the artifacts created by the most imaginative and innovative graduates of the art schools and colleges are eagerly snapped up as the antiques of the future.

Britain, which led the way in the mid-19th century, also pioneered attempts to foster good design in an infinite range of useful articles, from household appliances to postage stamps, through the medium of the government-sponsored Design Centre and the Council of Industrial Design. During World War II, when there was a shortage of materials and manpower, these schemes helped to develop the utility concept, which extended over the entire range of manufactured goods. At the time, "utility" was often equated with shoddy and second-rate, but in more recent times collectors have begun to appreciate the simple lines of the applied arts of the so-called austerity period.

There was a time when objects were collected for their own sakes; as examples of exquisite craftsmanship, beauty, or rarity. Perhaps the reason for collecting was nothing more than the charm of owning something of great age. At any rate, intrinsic worth was seldom of primary consideration. Nowadays, however, there is a tendency for the collector to be aware of values and to prize his possessions not only for their esthetic qualities, but also as investments.

Gone are the days of the great gentleman-collectors, such as Sloane, Cotton, Harley, Hunter, Hearst, and Burrell, whose interests covered every collectable medium and whose tastes were equally developed for paintings and incunabula as for coins and illuminated manuscripts.

Even the computer billionaires of the present day could scarcely emulate the feat of the late Andrew Mellon, who in the 1920s once purchased 33 paintings from the Hermitage for $19 million. But while there are very few private individuals, who could now afford to buy a Leonardo, a Rembrandt, or even a Van Gogh, there are millions of people throughout the world who have the leisure to specialize in some chosen field, and the surplus cash to acquire the material for their collections.

There are countless aficionados who have formed outstanding collections of porcelain, silver, prints, or glass, who have specialized in the products of individual potteries, or Depression glass, or Kilner paperweights, or Goss china.

At the lower end of the spectrum there are hundreds of different classes of collectable, from the frankly ludicrous, such as bricks, barbed wire, and lavatory chain-pulls, to the fetishistic, including whips and certain articles of ladies' apparel. There are also collectors of commemorative wares and even objects associated with one's profession, such as dental and medical instruments. The collecting virus is now endemic and insatiable.

Styles and Periods

Britain emerged as a world power in the early 18th century, after the brilliant successes of its forces in the War of the Spanish Succession. In later conflicts Britain rivaled France for the mastery of the colonial world, in India and the Western Hemisphere, and emerged triumphant in 1763.

The accession of the Hanoverian kings in 1714 increasingly involved Britain in European politics and artistic influences. Despite the Jacobite rebellions of 1715 and 1745, Britain enjoyed a long period of relative stability and rising prosperity. Greater affluence was reflected in the furniture, glass, silverware, and decorative arts of the period.

The Georgian era is conveniently divided into Early Georgian, covering the reigns of the first two Georges (1714–60), and Late Georgian, corresponding with the long reign of George III (1760–1820). The era as a whole witnessed a tremendous development in architecture, which in turn influenced styles in the applied and decorative arts. The Early Georgian period coincided with the zenith of the Baroque in Europe, with its emphasis on curves and scrolls in everything from the legs of tables to the handles of coffee-pots. Scallops and acanthus leaves decorated the corners and joints of furniture as well as the rims of vessels.

The craze for curved lines culminated in the 1730s with the rise of Rococo, a much lighter, more delicate style than Baroque and clearly a reaction against its tendency to the massive and fussy. The Italianate word was actually derived from two French terms – *rocaille* (rockwork) and *coquille* (shell). It arose out of the vogue for grottoes in landscape gardening and was characterized by floral swags and garlands as well as "C" and "S" curves in great profusion. Britain lagged behind the Continent so it was not until the middle of the century that the Rococo fashion reached its height in England. It lent itself very well to setting off Oriental motifs, later joined by Indian art forms and continued, in a more restrained form, right through to the end of the 18th century. In general Rococo represented a much lighter approach to form and decoration than the Baroque. By the end of the century, however, styles were becoming more eclectic, often blending the Rococo with the Neo-classical and even the Gothic, an artificial revival of certain medieval forms such as pointed arches.

In glassware this was the period of much lighter forms, encouraged by the Glass Excise Act of 1745, which taxed glass by weight. The massive drinking glasses fashionable in the period from 1685 to 1720 gave way to the more elegant baluster glasses with knopped stems as the century progressed, and by 1750 became much lighter. The deliberate use of air bubbles (which had originally occurred by accident) led to air twist stems of amazing intricacy.

The Prince of Wales, later King George IV, became Regent in 1811 as a result of the madness of his father, who lingered on until 1820. George IV reigned for a decade in his own right and was succeeded by his brother William IV (1830-37). It is convenient, however, to regard this entire period as Regency in terms of style. The Prince Regent's London residence was Carlton House, whose interior decoration was entrusted to the architect Henry Holland. Relying largely on French emigré craftsmen, Holland furnished Carlton House in a style that blended classical lines with sumptuous decoration. To this day "Carlton House" is a generic term to describe all manner of furniture in this Neo-classical style. Under the influence of such arbiters of taste as Thomas Hope, furniture gradually became more robust, with greater emphasis on comfort than

fragile elegance. In addition to the Oriental and Gothic motifs of an earlier generation, such diverse motifs as balloons, classical friezes, and Egyptian elements (inspired by the discovery of the Rosetta Stone and a new-found craze for the archaeology of the Pharaohs) began to make themselves felt. Exotic timbers, especially from the East Indies, became fashionable.

These influences spilled over into ceramics, silver and glass. Regency fashions did not die out abruptly with the accession of William IV in 1830, but already great social and political changes were sweeping over Britain. Although they were not crystallized until the middle of the century, it is customary in the world of fashion to speak of the Victorian era as if it had commenced seven years before the young queen ascended the throne in 1837. While fashion in ceramics, glass, and silver did not change much before the Great Exhibition of 1851, the styles, techniques, and even the materials of furniture had been undergoing radical alteration in previous decades. The rapid growth of economic prosperity, which came in the 1830s, stimulated a tremendous demand for furniture.

Although Victorian is used as a generic term for the applied and decorative arts of the 19th century, it had its European counterparts. The Biedermeier furniture and decor of mid-19th century Germany was long derided as conventional and unimaginative. Its name was derived from a fictional character, Gottlieb Biedermeier, a rather simple-minded, essentially philistine petit-bourgeois; an image that added to the derision surrounding it. But today its very solidity is now regarded as highly commendable, while there is much to delight the eye in many of the lesser pieces, especially the ceramics, glass, and silver. The French equivalent was Second Empire, roughly contemporary with the reign of Napoleon III (1852–71), and likewise unfairly dismissed by the generations that followed immediately, but is more valued now.

As the 19th century drew to a close, influences and developments in the applied and decorative arts became much more cosmopolitan. The French expression *fin de siècle* has come to be synonymous with decadence. The estheticism expressed by Oscar Wilde, J.K. Huysmans, and Robert de Montesquieu had its parallels all over Europe and even extended to America. The strange, exotic, luxuriant, and faintly decadent spirit of the times had its flowering in the sinuous lines of Art Nouveau. It was a period of eclecticism, when artists and designers drew freely on all the artistic styles and movements of previous generations from every part of the world, and often jumbled them together in a riotous compote. The craze for Japanese art and artifacts was predominant, but inspiration was also derived from the ancient civilizations of Greece and Rome, Persia, India, Peru, Mexico, Benin, and China. Nevertheless, it is significant that the German term for the turn of the century developments in the arts was *Jugendstil* or "youth style," implying vigor, freshness, originality, and modernity. The followers of the Arts and Crafts Movement, on the one hand, rejected modern mass-production techniques and sought to return to first principles, to handicrafts and inspiration from nature. The disciples of *Jugendstil*, on the other hand, did not spurn the machine if it could be used to their advantage, and they looked forward, in an age of speed and light, to producing works which would express the qualities of the age.

The major countries of Western Europe and the United States each had an important part to play in the development of the applied and decorative arts. In Britain, the desire for improvement in industrial design can be traced back to the Great Exhibition of 1051 and,

even earlier, to the Royal Commission on the Fine Arts in 1835. The Gothic Revival of the mid-19th century stimulated interest in medievalism, reflected in the religious overtones of the early work of William Morris, Philip Webb, and Edward Burne-Jones. It would be difficult to overestimate the importance of Morris to the artistic development of Britain in the late-19th century. Two important movements stemmed directly or indirectly from his teachings. One was the Arts and Crafts Movement of the 1880s, which aimed at bringing artists and craftsmen closer together, to raise standards of workmanship, and to put artistic pride into even the most mundane articles. The other was the Aesthetic Movement, founded on an elitist principle, which genuinely strove to raise standards of design and taste. On the continent of Europe, styles, which culminated in Art Nouveau, had their origins in France where two major artistic movements flourished in the last third of the century, Naturalism and Symbolism. Parallel developments in Belgium, Italy, and Spain, which fused in the 1890s, were enthusiastically adopted in England and given a distinctly British flavor before finding their way back across the Channel in the guise of *le style anglais*.

The Civil War of 1861–65 was no less traumatic for the United States than the German occupation and the Commune of 1870–71 were for France. The rapid expansion of industry, coupled with widespread immigration from Europe, changed the character of the country in the last three decades of the century. America ceased to be a pioneer land and in the aftermath of the Spanish-American War of 1898 assumed an imperial role. In the arts, as in politics, America now reached out to every part of the globe. Interest in the arts of China and Japan, of Latin America and Africa, were combined with the traditional styles, which were

themselves derived from the British, Dutch, and German of the colonial era or imported with the waves of European migration from the 1860s onwards. This blend of Oriental or pre-Columbian influences with the styles and techniques of Europe could be seen in the furniture, glassware, and ceramics of America at the turn of the century. These, especially art glass and studio pottery, found their way to Europe where they exerted a considerable influence on the applied arts of the present century.

The young architects and designers of the Chicago School revolutionized the design of buildings and furniture from the 1890s onwards. In Europe, the break with the old ideas was often more dramatic, as, for example, in the *Sezession* movement in Austria and Germany. The world of the arts and crafts was thrown into turmoil. Many new ideas and styles appeared; some were short-lived and have now become crystallized in the history of the period, but others contained the seeds that germinated in the 1920s and came to full maturity nearer the present day. Notably, the Bauhaus movement in Germany influenced the development of Art Deco in the 1920s with its rejection of the curvilinear extravagance of Art Nouveau. Geometric forms and bright primary colors were in tune with the Jazz Age.

Pitfalls and Plus Factors

Collectors, and not always beginners by any means, are often puzzled by the vast price differential between two objects, which are superficially similar. In some

LEFT: (Clockwise from top) A French sulphide, a St Louis weight, a Bohemian weight, a French flask, a miniature Baccarat weight, and a French millefiori weight.

cases there may be as many as a dozen criteria governing the value of an object: age, materials, type of construction, quality of craftsmanship, artistic or esthetic considerations, unusual technical or decorative features, the provenance of personal association, the presence or absence of makers' marks, dates, and inscriptions. These and other criteria vary in importance from one object to another, and may even vary within the range of a single category, at different periods or in certain circumstances. Visiting museums and stately homes or handling objects at sale previews, as well as studying all available specialist literature on any given subject, will help the aspiring collector to get a feel for a subject, but there is no shortcut to gaining expertise.

Above all, condition is the most problematic factor in assessing the worth of an object. Reasonable condition, of course, depends on the object and the degree to which damage and repairs are accepted by specialist collectors and dealers. The general rule is that where a piece is interesting and few collectors have one in their collection, a much damaged example will fetch a surprisingly good price. This often happens with early examples of glass from important factories, whereas a common piece will be virtually worthless. The failure to appreciate the effects on value of poor condition is one of the most common causes of the misunderstanding that arise between collectors and dealers.

The market value will also take into account the imponderables of where, when and how an article came on to the market. There is often a wide disparity in the sum that identical objects may fetch in a London saleroom, in a provincial auction, or a country house sale. The individual vagaries of the obsessiveness of two or more wealthy private collectors may grossly affect the auction prices of certain objects on a particular occasion, while absolutely identical objects can

(and sometimes do) fetch half these sums at other times in other places. Moreover, there is both a greater disparity between prevailing auction realizations and dealers' retail prices in general, and between the prices of one dealer and another, who are not always situated miles apart! Unfortunately, the collector cannot shop around before making a purchase. There are still bargains to be picked up; but all too often one finds that objects are outrageously overpriced in general antique or junk shops. Contrary to popular belief, some of the keenest bargains are still to be found in metropolitan antique shops and markets, where competition comes into play; conversely some of the most atrocious overpricing has been observed in provincial towns or the antique "boutiques" in tourist areas. There is no clearly definable regional pattern of pricing in the United Kingdom or the United States or anywhere else for that matter; this is something that collectors have to explore for themselves.

While a certain amount of judicious repair and restoration is permissible, fakery is reprehensible and usually detracts from whatever value the genuine part of the object may have had before it was tampered with. Unfortunately the dividing line between legitimate repair and outright faking is often a rather tenuous one; but the general principle is that any deliberate altering of an object to create something of greater value is a form of fraud. It occurs most often in furniture, where large but unfashionable and unsaleable pieces are dismembered and their timbers used to recreate small pieces, which with a bit of luck can be passed off as genuine articles. The other problem that besets the unsuspecting collector of antiques in general is reproduction. Although this is not so important in glass where early Victorian reproductions of 17th and 18th century styles are now regarded as antiques in their own right, there will obviously be quite a wide difference in the antiquarian value. This is also the case with early 20th-century reproductions of Louis Quinze. In all cases of doubt, it is recommended that the would-be purchaser get the advice of a reputable dealer or auctioneer. Legislation in many countries in recent years, such as the Trades' Descriptions Act in Britain, place a grave responsibility on the vendors and their agents to ensure that articles are properly described.

At the end of the day, the age-old maxim *caveat emptor* is as important as ever, but do not let this deter you from enjoying the quest for your chosen subject. All collectors make mistakes along the way; as long as they learn from the experience no great harm is done.

Glass

It often comes as a surprise to learn that glass has been around for thousands of years. As far back as 4000 B.C. the Egyptians were using molten glass to cover stone beads, and by 1500 B.C. had developed the technique of molding glass to produce small vessels. By the beginning of the Christian era glass blowing was perfected and thereafter quite large and elaborate jugs, jars and drinking glasses came into use. The Romans manufactured elegant glassware, although the quality gradually declined towards the end of the fourth century. Despite the fall of Rome to the barbarians, glass bottles and vessels for domestic or commercial use continued to be made during the Dark Ages, although this green glass was rough and unpretentious. Plate glass, essential for the manufacture of windows and mirrors, improved greatly from the 12th century onward.

In the Middle Ages, the finest traditions of glass were maintained in Islamic countries. It was from them that the art was reintroduced into western Europe, via Spain and especially Venice, which was the leading center of luxury glass from the 15th century onward and continues to rank very highly to this day. From Venice the art of fine glass gradually spread to other parts of Italy and then crossed the Alps to Germany (which developed crystal glass) and England (which pioneered lead glass). While crystal glass was hard and capable of being blown in very thin forms, English lead glass was generally much thicker and heavier and seen at its best in simple forms. Soda glass continued to be imported mainly from Venice throughout the Jacobean period, and examples in fine condition are now very expensive.

In 1664, the "Worshipful Company of Glass-sellers and Looking-glass Manufacturers" was incorporated and in the same year George Villiers, second Duke of Buckingham, obtained a patent to make glass. He established a factory at Vauxhall, London, and by the end of the 17th century the production of mirrors had expanded enormously. They continued to be relatively expensive, and it was not until about 1740 that they became at all plentiful. Thereafter they became increasingly popular, especially when extravagantly decorated in the Rococo style.

English preeminence in the field of lead glass was due to George Ravenscroft (1618–81), who for the first time obtained the silica needed for glassmaking from English instead of Venetian flints and added an oxide of lead called litharge. His glass was heavier than Venetian glass of the same period, but superior in brilliance and its remarkable light-dispensing quality. The simple and elegant designs of the late 17th and early 18th centuries showed the glass at its best, and the work of Ravenscroft and the glassmakers that followed him not only produced the first authentic English style in glassware but also reached the high point of English glass production for all time.

Collectors are unlikely to come across glasses produced in England before Ravenscroft's time, and would probably not recognize them as such if they did, for they were produced by continental craftsmen in a style barely distinguishable from that of Venice or l'Altare near Genoa. Most of the identifiable examples are now confined to museums, and if they come on to the market they would be extremely expensive.

Drinking Glasses

The earliest examples of modern European glass were produced by the Venetians, whose goblets and wine glasses were delicately blown and beautifully ornamented. From 1685, George Ravenscroft of London evolved a new and heavier type of glass containing lead oxide.

This "flint" glass is exceptionally rare, and fewer than a dozen wine glasses by Ravenscroft are in existence. As it was darker and heavier than the Venetian ware and took a long time to cool, flint glass was unsuitable for the light ornament so beloved of the Venetians. The English glassmakers, however, made the most of its dark beauty and produced wine glasses, which possess a simple charm and elegance. The earliest glasses (1690–1730) are huge by modern standards with large bowls whose generous capacity reflected the drinking habits of the times.

From the plain, straight-sided funnel evolved various fluted shapes, bell, waisted, and trumpet-bowls. These shapes were retained well into the 19th century, so the stems of drinking glasses are more important for the purpose of dating them. Predominant in the Queen Anne period was the baluster stem, upright or inverted. From about 1720 variety was added by the inclusion of knops, or shaped enlargements, which gave strength and beauty to the stem. Highly prized

Above: An engraved and polished armorial part glass table service, including decanters, tumblers, wine glasses, goblets and liqueur glasses, dating from 1900.

are drawn-stem glasses and those in which air bubbles were drawn out and twisted to form an internal "rope" of fine air lines. Other rare examples had a "tear" or elongated air bubble in the baluster.

Enameled glasses were very fashionable in Europe during the Rococo period, notably in Germany, which had a long tradition of beakers and tankards extravagantly decorated with armorial motifs and historical scenes. In England, the best enameled glass was produced in Bristol, London, and Newcastle. Glasses engraved for purely decorative or commemorative purposes rose to prominence in the second half of the 18th century. The ones that are particularly prized are the rose, "amen," and portrait glasses associated with the Jacobite movement after the failure of the 1745–46 rebellion.

Many new styles of glass, including experiments with colors, cutting, acid-etching, layering, and other decorative treatments, developed in the late 19th century, especially in the United States, under such names as Amberina, Agata, Peachbloom, Burmese, the iridescent Aurene, and Tiffany's Favrile. Loetz and Lobmeyr also started to make iridescent glass, while the Bohemian glassworks produced excellent luster wares and colored glasses. After 1900, iridescent glass went out of favor and there was a return to plainer glass with greater emphasis on elegant lines.

In more recent times excellent glassware has been produced in Scandinavia, notably by Kosta, Orrefors, and Reijmyre in Sweden. In Germany, the best glasses at the turn of the century were produced by Karl Kopping and Friedrich Zitzmann, paving the way for the glasses designed by Peter Behrens in the best Bauhaus tradition.

Decanters

Otherwise known as serving bottles or jugs, these vessels were developed in the third quarter of the 17th century. Hitherto wine was served direct from its own bottle at the table. The earliest decanters were fitted with handles but otherwise closely resembled the contemporary wine bottles. These so-called decanter jugs were straight-sided, round-shouldered vessels with a funnel-shaped, spouted neck carrying a loose-fitting stopper. Virtually all of the 17th-century examples of these decanter jugs are now in museum collections. For all practical purposes the decanters available to the collector commence with the early 18th century. Small decanters are less desirable than bottle-sized ones, while larger ones such as magnums and upwards are much sought after.

Decanters can be dated by their shapes. Up to 1730, most had straight octagonal sides, rounded shoulders, and a tall neck, and the presence of a handle is a major plus factor. From 1720 to 1745, bodies were deeply indented and broadly cruciform in section; cut glass ornament became fashionable in the 1730s. The shaft and globe decanter, which has a spherical body and a long, slim neck, was in vogue from 1745 to 1765, and the body is sometimes ringed with regular indentations known as Lynn molding. Engraved scenes fashionable at this time, and those with political motifs relating to James II or William of Orange are particularly desirable. Shouldered decanters, widest at the shoulders and tapering slightly towards the base, were produced between 1755 and 1770. In addition to engraving, if there is enameled ornament by the Beilbys this greatly enhances the value. In this period James Giles produced excellent decanters in colored glass with gilding and enameling, and examples in which the ornament is intact fetch very high prices.

Mallet decanters, with a wide base and sides tapering slightly towards the shoulders, with a short neck, were also fashionable from 1765 to 1775 and may be found in the same decorative styles as before. Later styles are: the Indian club, often with names of wines engraved on them (1765–90); tapered decanters (1780–1800); mold-blown decanters, often of Irish origin (1780–1840); diamond-molding in an overall pattern in flint glass (1800–30); heavy cut glass on bulbous shapes with elaborate collars (1810–40); pillar cutting on a vertical form (1830–50); Gothic style with elaborate cutting (1850–1900); cameo glass (1870–1900); molded or pressed Art Nouveau ornament (1895–1910); rectangular or cuboid with wheel-engraving (1900–30); and geometric patterns in Art Deco cocktail style (1920–40). Desirable features are three rings on a relatively short neck, a flat disc stopper, or a stopper in mushroom form with radial cutting. Other points to look for are unusual neck rings, such as the milled neck ring grained like the rim of a coin, the feathered neck ring tooled in the center to give a feathered effect, or the blade neck ring which has a triangular section.

Scent Bottles

Interest in perfumery reached its peak during the 17th and 18th centuries when insanitary conditions made some sort of sweet-smelling scent imperative. The manufacture of perfume developed into an art and went hand in hand with the skills of jewelers and gold-smiths in the production of vessels worthy of the precious liquid.

During this period, but particularly during the second half of the 18th century, countless tiny bottles were produced all over Europe. They continued in a less flamboyant manner throughout the 19th century

and many fine examples of modern scent bottles are produced by Lalique for Coty to this day.

Many different materials have been used, but glass is by far the commonest. The Venetian glass-blowers of the 17th century produced elegant scent bottles in colored glass. The Germans specialized in the use of *Milchglas*, an opaque white glass that was frequently decorated with flowers or figures in colored enamels and gilding. Italian glass-workers took their art to France and produced interesting bottles in colored or opaline glass, often formed into fancy shapes. Although the great glasshouse of Baccarat is best remembered for its paperweights it should be noted that it also produced many exquisite scent bottles with heavy bases incorporating *millefiori* patterns.

In England the manufacture of scent bottles is usually associated with Bristol whose merchants, by securing a monopoly of cobalt oxide exported from Silesia, gave the town the lead in the production of brilliant blue Bristol glass. The Bristol glassmakers also made scent bottles in emerald, amethyst, and opaque white glass in the latter part of the 18th century. The scent bottles were often beautifully cut and engraved. Those in opaque glass were usually decorated with enamel painting and embellished with gold or silver mounts.

Clear glass scent bottles can be dated to some extent by the cutting. Prior to about 1790, the glass was suitable only for cutting in shallow relief but after that date, especially in the Regency period, deep cutting was immensely popular.

Apsley Pellatt, one of the most original of English glass manufacturers in the early 19th century, invented a process for mounting glass paste cameos within the fabric of scent bottles, usually set off by deeply cut facetting. Where gold or silver mounts were used it may be possible to date scent bottles from their hallmarks, though many of them were unmarked if the mount was negligible in weight.

Other Forms and Other Places

Venice was not only the chief center of glass production in Europe from an early date, but also the place where the greatest variety of forms and styles developed. The glassware destined for the luxury markets of Europe was distinguished not only for its lightness and elegance, but in the application of many different colors, and the adroit employment of enamels and gilding to heighten decorative effect. Venice was also a major center for the production of ornamental bowls and vases as well as figurines, and these traditions continue to this day.

The glassware of Spain, not surprisingly, was strongly influenced by Islamic traditions. Beautiful colored glass in the Hispano-Mauresque tradition was produced in Andalusia at a relatively early period. Not only in the fabulous ornamentation of glass, but also in the production of distinctive vessels, the Spanish glassmakers excelled, and they were noted for their intricate glass baskets and toys of many kinds of colored glass. Opaque or milk glass was another speciality, often decorated in enamels.

In the lands of the Holy Roman Empire the chief center was in Bohemia (now the Czech Republic) and still an important source of glass of all kinds, but by the 16th-century glass factories had been established all over Germany and Austria. As well as fine, light glass in the Venetian style, manufactured by Italian craftsmen, the German factories developed their own distinctive styles. Notably these were the *Roemer*, a heavy drinking glass (from which we get the English word "rummer"); the *Stangenglas*, a tall, cylindrical vessel; and the *Humpen*. The latter was immensely fashionable with beer drinkers and extremely popular with collectors in its more elaborate forms, often richly decorated with armorial devices and commemorative inscriptions, which enhances the value considerably. In addition to enameling and gilding, the German glassmakers developed the art of engraving, carving, and cutting glass.

The glass produced in Holland tended to imitate Venice, England, Germany, and Bohemia in form and actual metal, but where it distinguished itself was in the exquisite decoration that evolved in the 17th and 18th centuries. As in Germany, there was a penchant for engraved glass, at first stippled by diamond point, but later produced by wheel. On the other hand, the glass from the Belgian factories was strongly influenced by their French counterparts.

In France, window glass was preeminent and exported to many other countries. This was the country in which stained glass for the windows in churches and chateaux made a tremendous impact, but concentration on this aspect of glass tended to lead to the neglect of more domestic forms, which were confined to simple designs executed in green glass. In the 16th century, however, Italian craftsmen settled in and around the town of Nevers and began producing glass toys fashioned from colored glass rods, and from this slowly developed the major industry it is today. Fine table glass was later produced in Lorraine, but in the 19th century the glassworks of Baccarat, Clichy and St Louis were preeminent, and later came the great work of the artist-manufacturers such as Daum, Gallé and Lalique, whose names are household words for exquisite glass to this day.

The manufacture of glass came relatively late to Scandinavia, and Swedish glass of the 18th and 19th centuries tends to be rather pale imitations of German forms. However, there was an extraordinary upsurge of glassmaking from the early 20th century onwards, and both useful and ornamental wares were produced in Denmark and Finland as well as Sweden. Scandinavian glass tends to be colorless or in pale shades of blue and green, and relies more on form and texture for its design. For many years it has been in the forefront of modern glass design.

A glassworks was established at Jamestown, Virginia, as long ago as 1608, operated by workmen from Germany and the Low Countries. This established the precedent for many of the later glassworks, which relied heavily on German and Bohemian technology. Apart from a vast range of domestic and commercial glass, the American factories led the world in the development of unusual color combinations and textures. This culminated in the late 19th century in the splendid art glass, often with names that are just as exotic, and which have survived in many cases to the present time.

Cameo and Cut Glass

Cameo glass developed in Britain in the late 19th century and was peculiar to that country. Cameo glass of a sort was also produced in France by Emile Gallé, but differed from its English counterpart in many respects. Cameo glass involved the revival of techniques known to the Romans and seen at their best in the famous Portland Vase. It consists of cased or flash glass, with several layers and usually incorporating an opaque glass on a colored ground with a matt finish. The cameo effect was achieved by carving, or otherwise removing, the outer layer to reveal the opaque glass underneath. The best and earliest cameo glass was engraved by hand, but towards the end of the century, when cameo glass increased in popularity, various mechanical processes were introduced. Cutting could

be done on a wheel, but more often decoration was applied in acid-resistant materials and the surrounding area then removed by immersion in acid.

The best examples of cameo glass include the various copies of the Portland Vase between 1873 and 1880. The Elgin Marbles at the British Museum were another source of inspiration and formed the character of English cameo glass, which was almost entirely classical in composition.

Cameo glass on a commercial basis, using acid-etching, was introduced by Thomas Webb in 1884. From then until 1911 Webb Cameo glass, with its white floral or classical motifs on a colored base, was exceedingly popular. These pieces were invariably stamped "Webb's Gem Cameo" and many examples in the 1890s also bore the date of manufacture. George and Thomas Woodall produced the best of the hand-engraved cameo glass for Webb. Stevens & Williams of Stourbridge also produced excellent cameo glass, either alone or in conjunction with J. & J. Northwood.

After 1900, there was a tendency towards more naturalistic motifs, with flowers and plants predominating, reflecting the fashion for Art Nouveau. English cameo glass declined in popularity in about 1910 and production appears to have ceased during World War I, although there were sporadic attempts to revive it in the 1920s.

It was applied mainly to vases, bowls, and centerpieces, though it may also be found in decanters and drinking glasses. From about 1884 Emile Gallé began producing a type of cameo glass in which the

RIGHT: Two cameo glass bowls by Gallè, dating from around 1900.

decoration was cut by a wheel into the various layers of colored glass. Gallé also adopted acid-etching in the 1890s to cope with the demand for cameo glass, mainly from the Near East and Mediterranean markets. Cameo glass is sometimes confused with a white enamel-painted glass, of German or Bohemian origin, which was designed to compete against cameo glass for public favor.

The cutting and facetting of glass surfaces to give them a diamond sparkle has been widely practiced for centuries. This was raised to an art form in the late 19th century, when heavy rock crystal was deeply carved to produce high-relief pictures on the sides of vessels in imitation of Oriental jade. Intaglio, the opposite of cameo, involved cutting the design into the glass using copper or stone wheels; a technique developed at Stourbridge in the 1890s.

Paperweights

Although credit for inventing glass paperweights must go to the Venetians, who revived the Egyptian art of glass mosaic known as *millefiori* (literally translated as "thousand flowers"), the French undoubtedly raised it to a fine art. These enchanting glass globes with their delicate and intricate patterns were subsequently made in Britain and continue to this day by such companies as Whitefriars, Strathearn, and Caithness Glass.

From the collector's viewpoint the most desirable paperweights are those which were produced at three French factories in the middle of the 19th century. The esteem in which the weights of St Louis, Baccarat, and Clichy are held is justified on account of their superlative workmanship, vivid coloring, and intricate designs. The *millefiori* patterns were built up of short lengths of bundles of glass canes laid on a bed plate.

Each bundle might contain anything from six to 50 canes and up to 100 bundles would comprise the "set-up" of a paperweight with an average diameter of 3 in. (7.5cm). Various motifs other than florets were often incorporated, featuring animals, insects, or dancing figures.

Although scattered patterns were the most popular, other types of *millefiori* were used. Comparatively rare are the mushrooms on which the central tufts of millefiori are surrounded by concentric bands entwined in a latticed pattern. Other types are known as sulphides or incrustations, in which a cameo portrait of some celebrity was incrusted in the glass. *Millefiori* may also be found arranged in a serpentine pattern; these "snakes" were a speciality of the St Louis factory. Other types include bouquets and overlays, the latter having windows ground and polished into the sides and top of the globe.

Although the classic period for these small bibelots was from 1842 to 1870, they remained popular and were revived or adapted in many other parts of the world. Paperweights in the classic genre of Baccarat, Clichy, and St Louis continued to be produced at the turn of the century. However, this was a sporadic business and such weights (attributed to Pantin and other factories) are now thought to have been "end of day" wares made by individual craftsmen and not intended for the commercial market. They include the Pantin giant salamander weights, which are now the most sought after of all.

In England, the production of paperweights was conducted intermittently by the Whitefriars glassworks, using traditional *millefiori* patterns. J. Kilner & Sons of Yorkshire produced large bottle-glass weights, containing floral or plant motifs composed of fine bubbles, from 1830 to the 1920s. There has been a tremendous revival of paperweight production in the past half century, notably in Belgium, the Czech Republic, the United States, and Scandinavia, which has greater emphasis on the form, color, and texture of the glass itself, as well as the use of carving and engraving to enhance decoration.

Mirrors

Silvered looking-glasses were imported from Europe until the late-17th century and were extremely expensive. English mirrors date from 1665 when the Duke of Buckingham established a glassworks at Vauxhall, London. The earliest mirrors are relatively small, owing to the problems of producing plate glass without surface distortion. Later mirrors vary enormously in size, shape, and purpose. Age itself is of relatively little importance in assessing value, as the bulk of the value lies in the frame rather than the glass.

The earliest collectable type, around 1700, had a plain rectangular pine frame veneered with walnut, but by 1710 mirrors were beveled and often shaped with a rounded top. More elaborate mirrors were decorated in the Dutch manner and had marquetry borders and floral motifs. The most desirable types in this early period have gilded and carved crests. As the century progressed frames became increasingly elaborate, enriched with carving, gilding, and burnishing. A cheaper version used gesso, plaster of Paris carved in low relief, and gilding. Mahogany frames decorated with giltwood carving were popular from 1730, and were usually in the extravagant Rococo style. Tops may be straight with rounded corners or decorated with broken or swan's neck pediments. The most desirable examples have crested tops, with "C" and "S" scrolls in the borders, foliage, and animal motifs.

More formal, though delicately symmetrical, forms reflected the neoclassicism of the late 18th century. Comparatively plain mirrors with oval frames were embellished with classical motifs, such as urns and acanthus leaves worked on gilt or painted wood. During the Regency period circular mirrors with a convex surface were in vogue, framed in giltwood with restrained decoration. Similar mirrors surmounted by an eagle, a Napoleonic affectation, are highly desirable on account of their American appeal.

Other Regency mirrors are rectangular with a decorative panel at the top, often in combination with carved giltwood and plaster composition material. Decorative forms include a brass lattice-work grille or Wedgwood jasper plaques inset. Similar mirrors with a glass painting in the top panel are very desirable. Early 19th century European girandoles with irregular shapes surrounded by lavishly carved giltwood frames were sometimes produced in pairs. Late 19th-century wall mirrors with wooden frames were sometimes decorated with *repoussé* copper, pewter, and enamel decoration in the Art Nouveau manner.

Small upright mirrors mounted on swivels between vertical supports with a drawer or bank of drawers underneath came into fashion at the beginning of the 18th century and sat on dressing-tables or tallboys. The style of these toilet mirrors usually parallels that of the wall mirrors of the corresponding period. Examples with japanned woodwork are particularly desirable. Cheval glasses are mirrors on swivel mounts without the base cabinet found in toilet mirrors. They may be quite small and mounted on bracket feet for display on top of a dressing-table, and the majority date from 1750 onwards.

Façon de Venise Goblet
16th century

The flared funnel bowl of this goblet is lightly molded with an overall "beech-nut" pattern, and is believed to come from the 16th-century workshop of Sebastian Höchstetler. Good quality glass made in the Venetian fashion was produced in Germany, the Low Countries, and England in the 16th and 17th centuries.

Façon de Venise Flute
16th century

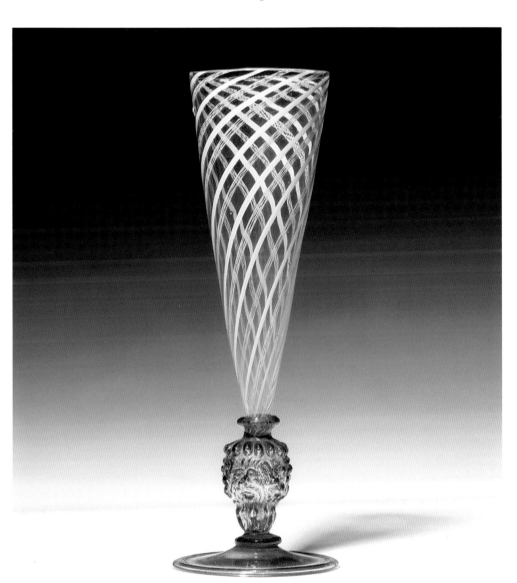

**A t a
G l a n c e**

Date: 16th century
Origin: Venice or
Low Countries
Brief description:
A *Façon de Venise*
latticinio flute.

This flute provides a
fine example of early
latticinio, *the latticework
of opaque glass threads
worked throughout the
body. Made in* vetro a
retorti, *literally translated
as "glass with a twist,"
the slender flared bowl
has alternating spiral
single white threads and
gauze cable. It is supported on a molded oviform
knop stem with lion's
masks alternating with
flowerheads, on a folded
conical foot.*

Façon de Venise Goblets
17th century

At a Glance

Date: 17th century
Origin: Low Countries
Brief description: (left to right) *Façon de Venise* winged wine glass, Venetian *latticinio* winged goblet in *vetro a penne*, a *Façon de Venise* serpent-stemmed goblet with a bell bowl, and a *Façon de Venise* serpent-stemmed goblet with a deep funnel bowl.

Glass of this type is characterized by the use of vivid coloring as well as the extravagant decoration of the stems. Bowls were either plain or ornamented with diamond engraving.

Façon de Venise Goblet
c.1650

At a Glance

Date: c.1650
Origin: Southern Netherlands
Brief description:
A Façon de Venise serpent-stemmed goblet.

The type of glass is known as vetro a serpenti, translated as "snake glass," from the stem formed of coiled tubing. The generous funnel of a clear white tint is set upon a merese (a type of collar with a sharp edge), and the stem is flanked by a pair of sea serpents enclosing white threads, the whole mounted on a folded conical foot.

Dutch *Roemer*
mid 17th century

At a Glance

Date: mid 17th century
Origin: Holland
Brief description: A large *roemer* in light-green glass.

The convex bowl is supported on a hollow cylindrical stem applied with four rows of raspberry prunts, on a high trailed conical foot. Developed in the 15th century, it attained its greatest popularity between 1685 and 1825. This Dutch version dates from the mid-17th century.

Tankard
1606

At a Glance

Date: 1606
Origin: Germany
Brief description:
A German silver-gilt mounted enameled tankard.

The tankard itself was of Bohemian manufacture but the decoration could have been applied anywhere in southern Germany. The glass body is enameled with an owl painted in blue, shown spinning wool. Both the owl and the action of spinning symbolize wisdom. The tankard is decorated with sprays of lily-of-the-valley and foliate scrolls in several colors. The gilt-metal domed cover is inset with a small medal of the Emperor Charles V, within three oval cartouches chases with landscapes and buildings ornamented with fruit, while the thumbpiece is in the form of a caryatid.

Puzzle Goblet
17th century

At a Glance

Date: 17th century
Origin: Germany
Brief description:
A green-tinted *Scherzgefas*
(puzzle goblet).

The waisted funnel bowl has a
detachable top in the form of
a stag, mounted on a central
column. The hollow stem has
a large knop with four aper-
tures, which had to be covered
to prevent the liquid
spurting everywhere.

Humpen
1723

At a Glance

Date: 1723
Origin: Germany
Brief description: An enameled *humpen* or *pasglas*.

Tall, cylindrical beakers with a slightly projecting base, known as humpen, are noted for their elaborate enameled and gilt decoration. The vast majority of them were produced in Germany, Bohemia, and Silesia from the middle of the 16th until the late 18th centuries.

Kurfürstenhumpen
mid 18th century

At a Glance

Date: Mid 18th century
Origin: Germany
Brief description: A German Kurfürstenhumpen, so-called because the cylindrical body was decorated in enamels and gilded with equestrian portraits of the Seven Electors of the Holy Roman Empire.

These elaborately ornamented glasses originated in the 16th century, but this example is a remarkably late efflorescence, believed to have been decorated by a porcelain Hausmaler such as Mayer of Pressnitz.

Punch Bowl, Glasses, and Jug
c.1690

At a Glance

Date: c. 1690
Origin: England
Brief description: A punch bowl, drinking glass, water jug, and two custard glasses.

Early attempts to produce crystal glass in England were unsuccessful because of its extreme fragility, and the few surviving examples from the 1670s invariably show signs of "crizzling." By 1677, however, George Ravenscroft had solved the problem by adding lead oxide. After his patent expired in 1681 other glassmakers adopted his formula, with spectacular results. The slow-cooling properties of lead crystal meant that the slender forms of Venetian glass could no longer be used, and much heavier, chunkier forms evolved in their place. This is clearly evident in the punch bowl, the lower part molded with "nipt diamond waies," above a domed and folded foot molded in a canopy of a similar design.

Silesian Goblet and Drinking Glass
c.1745

At a Glance

Date: c.1745
Origin: Silesia
Brief description: A Silesian engraved goblet with matching cover, and a drinking glass of similar form.

The engraving of glass spread from Nuremberg to Silesia in 1690 when a cutting-mill was established at Hermsdorf to enable the Silesian court engraver Friedrich Winter to work on glass. Winter produced a remarkable range of tall covered goblets renowned for deep undercutting and carving in the round, as well as the very finely detailed engravings of buildings and flowers, such as appear on these two glasses. The fluted ogee bowls are engraved with monograms below coronets flanked by scrolling leaves and flowers.

Composite-stemmed Glass
c.1700–1775

At a Glance

Date: c.1700–1775
Origin: England
Brief description: A rare composite-stemmed glass of English manufacture, but engraved in Holland.

The drinking glass is of an unusual design, with a funnel bowl and a very elaborate stem. The stem has a knop enclosing oblique air bubbles above three annular knops on top of an inverted baluster section enclosing a broad white opaque air-twist thread. In turn, this has a spiraling thread around a balustroid gauze core, with a basal knop above a conical foot. The chief interest of this glass, however, lies in its engraving. The bowl is decorated with an elaborate rocaille scroll above a tied wreath. Below is an altar with a heart surrounded by doves and flanked by two floral cornucopiae. The reverse is inscribed in Dutch Ik bemin maar Een ("I only love one") alongside a polished eye, symbolizing love and friendship.

Wineglasses
mid 18th century

At a Glance

Date: Mid 18th century
Origin: Europe
Brief description: A group of three wineglasses.

On the left is a Saxon wineglass whose inverted conical bowl is on a faceted knopped stem and circular folded foot, engraved with a band of strapwork, feathers, and pendant garlands. In the center is a Bohemian red twist glass whose inverted conical bowl is spiral-molded as a shell, the knopped stem enclosing red latticinio threads on a circular folded foot. On the right is a German goblet (probably Silesian) whose inverted conical bowl has a flaring lower section and a faceted stem on a circular foot, bearing the crowned monogram "DAAC" within strapwork and foliate scrolls. The back of the glass is engraved with a basket of fruit within similar strapwork.

Tall Glasses
c.1760

The German glassmakers excelled in the production of tall glasses, extravagantly engraved with arms and landscapes. The Pokal or covered glass on the left was the ideal medium for all kinds of commemorative pieces. Notably the so-called confinement glasses, engraved with pictures of new-born infants, were designed to contain a mixture of nourishing eggs, sugar, and alcohol to build up the strength of the mother, and were the origin of the beverage advocaat. The goblet on the right bears the arms of the Duchy of Lauenstein, engraved above a band of matt stiff leaves, and stands on a faceted knop and baluster above a domed and folded foot.

Armorial Glass
c.1760–1830

At a Glance

Date: c.1760–1830
Origin: Bohemia
Brief description: A selection of Bohemian armorial glass.

The tradition of engraved armorial glass continued in Bohemia for many years. This group of stemmed wineglasses, goblets, and beakers dates between 1760 and 1830 and illustrates the range of engraving, deep-cutting, and faceting that continued to distinguish glass from this region.

Wineglasses
mid 18th century

In this period there was a fashion for glasses of relatively small capacity with drawn-trumpet bowls set on beaded, shoulder-knopped stems, which terminated in a basal knop on conical feet.

Topographical Beaker
c.1813

At a Glance

Date: c.1813
Origin: Austria
Brief description: A Viennese transparent enameled topographical beaker, decorated by Gottlob Mohn, dated 1813 and depicting Heidelberg am Neckar.

This is a splendid example of the topographical beakers hand-painted by this artist during the Gothic Revival in the early years of the 19th century.

Wineglasses
c.1765

At a Glance

Date: c.1765
Origin: England
Brief description: A group of wineglasses with color twist stems.

These glasses vary widely in value, depending on the color and intricacy of the decoration in the stem. Jacobite glasses were popular with certain factions in the 18th century and were designed for toasting "the King over the water" (the deposed James II and later his son and grandson, the Old Pretender, and Bonnie Prince Charlie respectively).

Armorial Wineglass
c.1765

The funnel bowl is enameled in
yellow, heightened in iron-red,
black and white with gilding,
and the arms are garnished with
trailing foliage and fruiting vine.
Enameled glasses attributed to
brother and sister, William and
Mary Beilby (1749–97), are
highly desirable. This remarkable couple were the children
of William Beilby (1705–65),
a goldsmith of Durham who
moved with his family to
Newcastle in 1760. At first
William and Mary worked for
the Dagnia-Williams glassworks
before branching out on their
own.

Enameled Goblet
c.1765–75

At a Glance

Date: c.1765–75
Origin: England
Brief description: Four wineglasses attributed to William Beilby.

William's earliest glasses are signed "W. Beilby junr." But the suffix was dropped after the death of his father. Glasses by Mary are relatively rare, as her promising career was cut short by a stroke in 1774.

The glass on the left shows an enameled bowl with fruiting vine and foliage (c.1775). Three figures in a boat flanked by trees and shrubs on islands with pendant foliage can be seen on the glass next to it (c.1765). The other two (c.1765) show a sportsman aiming his gun at a duck in flight, a dog at his side, and (right) the unusual subject of an obelisk surmounted by an urn in a landscape.

Enameled Beakers
c.1815–30

At a Glance

Date: c.1815–30
Origin: Vienna
Brief description: A group of Viennese enameled beakers known as *Ranftbecher*.

This type of low beaker with a tapering or waisted body stood on a thick-cut cogwheel base and was invariably richly ornamented with enameling and gilding. Such beakers were immensely fashionable in the Biedermeier period. The best pieces were decorated by Anton Kothgasser (1769–1851), a celebrated Viennese miniaturist, who also decorated porcelain and stained glass. These beakers were lavishly decorated with genre scenes, landscapes, and famous landmarks, such as Schönbrunn Palace (shown on the second beaker from the right).

Theresienthal Glasses
early 20th century

At a Glance

Date: Early 20th century
Origin: Bavaria
Brief description: A part set of Theresienthal gilt and enamel glasses by K. Wilhelm Warhorst.

These glasses show the range of sizes from the tiny liqueur glass (center) to the tall champagne glass and the waisted beaker (far right). Benedikt von Poschinger established a glassworks at Theresienthal in the Bayerischer Wald, Bavaria in 1836, but it sprang to fame under Benedikt's son Ferdinand (1815–67) and its reputation for glass of the highest quality was maintained by his son Ferdinand Benedikt who was in control from then until 1921. Latterly the company also produced some fine pieces of iridescent art glass in the style of Gallé and Tiffany.

English Bottles with Pressed-glass Seals
1720–30

At a Glance

Date: 1720–30
Origin: England
Brief description: A group of early English bottles with pressed-glass seals bearing the monograms of their owners.

Bottles with slender necks fitted with corks or stoppers as containers for wine and other liquids have existed since Roman times and may be found in many different shapes (globular, cylindrical, pear-shaped, hexagonal, or square) as well as in glass of many different colors and consistencies. The more collectable varieties, however, emerged in the late 17th and early 18th centuries. England was a major center of bottle-making from about 1650, producing bottles that superseded the earlier and unreliable earthenware bottles. English bottles are classified by their shapes, from the "shaft and globe," the "onion shape," and then the "slope and shoulder" style, which preceded the type with a cylindrical body in use from 1750 to the present day. Interest in early bottles, such as this group from the period 1720–30 lies in the pressed-glass seals affixed to their sides, bearing the monograms of their owners and often including a date as well.

Silver-mounted Glass
19th century

At a Glance

Date: 19th century
Origin: Europe
Brief description: Claret jugs,
cut-glass decanter, perfume
bottles, and jugs.

Glass was combined with silver
for decorative and utilitarian
purposes, both for ornamental
effect and practicality. Claret
jugs, fitted with a lid, were
sometimes mounted with a
collar, lid, and handle of silver,
as in the examples shown on
the left of this picture. In other
cases the use of silver was more
restrained, as in the cut-glass
decanter (right). Perfume bottles
(below right) were often fitted
with a silver top, while even
quite small items, such as the
group of the set of Austro-
Hungarian tapered jugs (lower
left) were sometimes mounted
with silver rims or collars. As the
silver bears assay marks, such
glassware can be precisely dated
and assigned to a specific town,
although the glass itself may be
of an earlier period.

Irish Glassware
18th century

At a Glance

Date: 18th century
Origin: Ireland
Brief description:
Two ship's decanters, claret jug, pitcher, and a pair of cut-glass punch bowls.

Although it has been claimed that glass was briefly manufactured in Dublin in about 1585, the Irish glass industry did not become established until the 1780s when the ban on importing glass from Ireland was lifted. British manufacturers took advantage of relocating to Ireland to avoid the high rates of duty imposed in England under the Excise Acts of 1745 and 1777. The item on the extreme left in the picture is an Irish clear-glass ship's decanter of about 1810. It has a compressed pear-shaped body with ribbed sides, a triple-ringed neck, and a rosette-cut mushroom stopper. On the extreme right is a Brierley ship's decanter, so-called on account of the exaggeratedly broad flat body designed to remain steady in a ship pitching through the sea. Alongside stands an English etched claret jug (third from left) and an Anglo-Irish cut-glass pitcher of about 1800 (fourth from left). The picture also includes a pair of late 18th century cut-glass punch bowls.

Stourbridge Jug
c.1880

At a Glance

Date: c.1880
Origin: England
Brief description: Stourbridge, engraved jug attributed to Joseph Keller.

This oviform (egg-shaped) jug is engraved with four egrets among grasses, and another in flight. The slender neck is engraved with leaves below a beaded band and flowering prunus, while the handle is decorated with a band of ovolos and the spreading foot engraved with prunus. This jug dating about 1880 was produced at Stourbridge, Worcestershire, a town associated with glassmaking in England since the 1560s when craftsmen from Lorraine settled there, and still a major center of the industry. Joseph Keller is believed to be the designer of this jug.

Stourbridge Glassware
c.1900

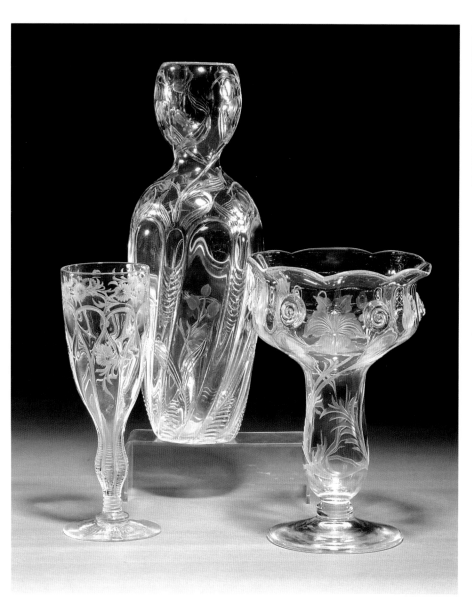

At a Glance

Date: c.1900
Origin: England
Brief description:
A Stourbridge decanter, vase, and wineglasses in matching designs.

Among the firms that are associated with Stourbridge glass are Stuart & Sons, Webb, Corbett, and Stevens & Williams. The latter is believed to have produced this group of glassware in the finest Art Nouveau tradition of about 1900. A decanter, vase, and wineglasses in matching designs, intaglio-engraved in rock crystal fashion with flowers and buds on tall stems and leaves between applied swirls, are typical of the curvilinear style of the turn of the 19th century.

English Scent Bottles
c.1830

At a Glance

Date: c.1830
Origin: England
Brief description: A group of English scent bottles showing a range of sizes and styles.

Special bottles designed to contain perfumes were produced with a very tiny opening to prevent the escape of the precious liquid, and then fitted with a correspondingly tight stopper. Essentially the techniques of making such bottles were the same as those for wine bottles, but on a much smaller scale, and calling for much greater precision. Because they were always regarded as a fashion accessory they were invariably lavished with ornament in the prevailing styles. This group of English scent bottles includes (center) a sulphide bottle of flattened oviform shape set with a sulphide (glass-paste) cameo portrait of King George IV, and decorated with alternating patterns of fine diamonds and polished pillar flutes. It was the work of Apsley Pellat (1791–1863), who owned the Falcon Glassworks at Southwark, London.

French Glassware
mid 19th century

This group of French glassware from the middle of the 19th century includes a pair of tall vases and an engraved dish, as well as a pair of green scent-bottles with matching stoppers. The globular bodies have been gilded with scattered stars, while the waisted necks have richly gilt everted rims with matching decoration on the stoppers.

At a Glance

Date: mid 19th century
Origin: France
Brief description: A group of French glassware.

Daum Perfume Bottle and Vase
c.1900

*The sky blue mottled glass of
both objects is enameled with a
naturalistic landscape. The perfume bottle with matching stopper bears the mark Daum, Nancy
with the cross of Lorraine and
initial AR. Antonin Daum co-
founder of the glassworks was
vice-president of the Nancy
School of Art from its inception
in 1903, and was an influential
figure in the development of Art
Nouveau glass.*

Lalique Scent Bottle
c.1925

At a Glance

Date: c.1925
Origin: France
Brief description: A clear and frosted scent bottle and stopper in graduating red to amber hues molded in low relief in the shape of a butterfly with outstretched wings, its body modeled as a woman.

Entitled "La Phalène," this bottle is a typical example of Lalique's hybrid-human creations inspired by some of the jewels which he produced in the early 1890s. Similar bottles with a triangular section were designed about 1914 by Lalique's contemporary, Lucien Gaillard.

Irish Bowls and Loving-cup
c.1780–1825

At a Glance

Date: c. 1780–1825
Origin: Ireland
Brief description: A pair of bowls and a covered two-handled loving-cup, all cut with bands of facets beneath wide bands of hobnail within diamond ornament.

The heyday of fine Irish glass was between 1780 and 1825 when the first Irish glass excise duty was imposed. It was made at Dublin, Belfast, Cork, and Waterford and was characterized by its heavy lead-glass body, ideally suited to wheel-engraving and deep cutting. Most Irish glass cannot be assigned to a specific factory, but it is characterized by its weight, form, and elaborate cutting. The cut circular bowl on the left had a triple annulated knop stem and a circular sunray foot.

British Glass and Rummers
1830s

At a Glance

Date: 1830s
Origin: Britain
Brief description: The picture shows examples of British glass dating from the 1830s, decorated with an over-all hobnail pattern (lower).

Glass decorated with cuts, grooves, and facets to catch the light and enhance the sparkle and brilliance of the vessel can be traced back to the 8th century BC, but it was raised to the status of high art from the late 17th century and attained its greatest splendour in the early 19th century when reduction in taxes and duties permitted the return to much heavier bodies. Behind are two large cut and engraved rummers, with bucket bowls bearing monograms surrounded by foliage. They are chiefly of interest for the silver groat (fourpence) coins of King William IV, dated 1836, which are embedded in the knopped stems.

British Cut-glass Vessels
early 19th century

This group of British glass shows several fine examples: (from left to right) a water jug with loop handle and a fluted body with alternate diamond-cut panels, and a star-cut base; a water jug with loop handle and fluted shoulders above a broad band of alternate diamond-cut lancets, and panels of polished circles on a strawberry field; a water jug of a more elaborate rococo pattern; and a small mounded glass water jug with an overall strawberry pattern.

Bohemian Goblet
c.1840

At a Glance

Date: c.1840
Origin: Bohemia
Brief description: A stained-ruby goblet and cover engraved by August Boehm at Meisterdorf.

The cylindrical bowl of this goblet has been carved and engraved with an elaborate battle scene at Lipan showing the last battle of the Hussite War in 1434. The goblet is mounted on a spreading octagonal foot with star-cut base.

Two-handled Vase and Goblet
c.1860/1880

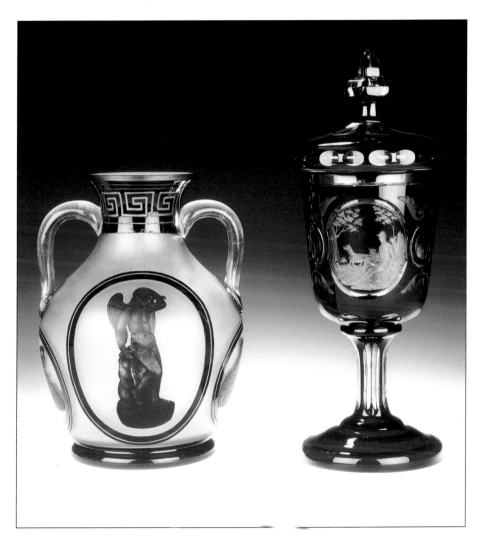

At a Glance

Date: c.1860/1880
Origin: North Bohemia
Brief description: An overlay two-handed vase engraved by Franz Zach (c.1860) and a Bohemian engraved ruby-flash goblet and cover, (c.1880).

In both pieces, layered glass of contrasting colors has been employed. The outer layer is cut away to form low relief figures and ornament.

Bohemian Circular Dish
c.1885

Josef Lobmeyr (1792–1855) founded a glassworks in Vienna in 1823 and the business was continued by his sons Josef (1828–64) and Ludwig (1829–1917). Stefan Rath (1876–1960), Lobmeyr's nephew, founded a branch factory a Steinschönau in Bohemia. Lobmeyr Senior restored cut and engraved glass to its former pre-eminence, and this tradition was later maintained by Rath, employing the finest Bohemian engravers such as Ullmann, Carl Pietsch, and Franz Knochel, all at Steinschönau.

Wiener Werkstatte Liqueur Set
c.1909–1916

At a Glance

Date: c.1909–1916
Origin: Austria
Brief description: A seven-piece liqueur set by the Wiener Werkstätte, attributed to Otto Prutscher and comprising two decanters and five glasses. The cylindrical bowls of the glasses and decanters are overlaid in amethyst glass and carved with geometrical motifs.

The Wiener Werkstätte (Vienna workshops) were founded in 1903 by Josef Hoffmann (1870–1935) and Koloman Moser (1868–1918) with the financial backing of Fritz Wärndorfer, the financier and patron of the Sezession movement. The chief aim of the workshops was to bring the artist or designer closer to the craftsmen and technicians entrusted with the execution of the design and as far as possible the designer was encouraged to be his own craftsman.

Scent Flasks
c.1887

At a Glance

Date: c.1887
Origin: England
Brief description: Two silver-mounted atomizer scent flasks, the silver by Middleton Chapman of London, 1887.

The globular bodies are overlaid in white opaque glass and carved with meandering sprays of apple blossom topped by false gadroon ornament at the shoulder. The underlying glass is blue or amber.

Gallé Cameo Vases
c.1900

At a Glance

Date: c.1900
Origin: France
Brief description: Three mold-blown cameo vases by Emile Gallé.

Emile Gallé (1846–1904) was leader of the Nancy School in the applied arts at the turn of the 19th century. By 1897 he was melting pieces of different colored glass into the basic glass body then carving and acid-etching to produce double-overlay decoration. Unlike most of his contemporaries, Gallé signed his works in gilt or brown enamel.

Gallé Vases
c.1890–1900

In the true spirit of Art Nouveau, Gallé went to nature for inspiration and carved flowers, trees, aquatic plants, snails, shells, wisteria, ferns, and occasional landscapes on his vases.

Gallé Coupe
c.1900

At a Glance

Date: c.1900
Origin: France
Brief description. A Gallé cameo glass coupe decorated with berries and foliage.

Unlike silver, glass usually presents many problems of attribution because so little of it is marked. Gallé, however, was always proud of his own creations and invariably signed his works putting the cameo mark of his surname on the base, usually in gilt or brown enamel in his own hand.

Gallé Cameo Glasses
c.1900

Apart from the distinctive style of cameo ornamentation, Gallé delighted in creating unusual shapes, and these vases with their tall slender cylindrical necks on extremely squat, almost flat circular bodies are typical examples.

Gallé Cameo Vase
c.1902

At a Glance

Date: c.1902
Origin: France
Brief description: Gallé vase with floral motif in dark red glass on a pink opaque ground.

A Gallé vase of a more conventional shape is this tapered cameo vase of about 1902. By the time of his death in 1904 his workshop had become a highly successful business with a considerable output, though quality was never sacrificed to quantity. After Gallé's death, the business was operated under the guidance of his friend Victor Prouvé and glass made in that decade (1904–14) continued to bear Gallé's signature, preceded by a small star. Production was halted on the outbreak of World War I.

Daum Table Lamp
c.1891

At a Glance

Date: c.1891
Origin: France
Brief description: A Daum carved and acid-etched double-overlay table lamp with a wrought iron base.

The glassworks operated at Nancy by the brothers Jean-Louis Auguste and Jean-Antonin Daum was inspired by the success of Gallé to diversify out of the more conventional and useful wares into decorative pieces from about 1891 onwards. Their wares bear the wheel-carved signature Daum Nancy with the cross of Lorraine. They produced tea and coffee services, but their lamps are very desirable.

Lalique Car Mascots
c.1925

It was in that year that Lalique diversified into yet another highly lucrative market, producing distinctive mascots for the motorcars driven by the super rich. These mascots, molded, carved, and acid-etched in clear glass with a slight bluish tinge, were soon regarded as the quintessential motoring accessory and in more recent years have become eminently collectable in their own right.

Lalique Car Mascot
c.1945

Later car mascots tended to abandon the original almost colorless glass for something more flamboyant. This model dates to the immediate post World War II period but shortly before Lalique's death. After 1945 the business was continued by his son Marc under the name of Cristallerie Lalique et Cie, but pieces, though still signed, omitted the initial R.

Lalique Powder Box
c.1900

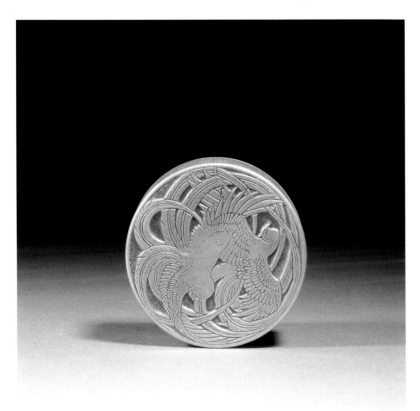

At a Glance

Date: c.1900
Origin: France
Brief description: A powder box in glass and gilt bronze entitled "Fleurs d'Amour" (love's flowers), manufactured by Lalique for the cosmetic firm of Roger et Gallet of Paris.

Although Lalique's involvement with the cosmetic industry was mainly through the perfume bottles he created for Coty, he also produced scent bottles and powder boxes for other companies. Because they are not so well-known they have been relatively overlooked but are now attracting the serious attention of collectors.

Pennell Glass Bowl
1991

At a Glance

Date: 1991
Origin: England
Brief description: "Myth Making," an engraved glass bowl by Ronald Pennell.

The motif has been wheel-engraved on a hand-blown glass bowl. The rose-tinted glass shows a man walking his dog, a Harpy rising in flights and a rhinoceros rushing into the mythical future. A fine piece showing that the art is still flourishing.

Gallé Goblet
c.1900

At a Glance

Date: c.1900
Origin: France
Brief description: An internally decorated, *marquetry-sur-verre* and wheelcarved *"verre parlant"* glass goblet.

The goblet is inlaid using the marquetry-sur-verre *technique to depict one orange and two purple fall crocuses, all blossoms finely carved with detailing.*

Venetian Tazza
17th century

At a Glance

Date: 17th century
Origin: Venice
Brief description: A 17th century Venetian latticinio tazza decorated with vertical bands of opaque white thread and gauze, the shallow bowl supported on a clear merese above a knopped baluster section and thick clear merese on a conical foot.

The Venetians pioneered this form of glass decoration, in this case vetro a retorti *with twists embedded in clear glass.*

Venini Decorative Glassware
mid 20th century

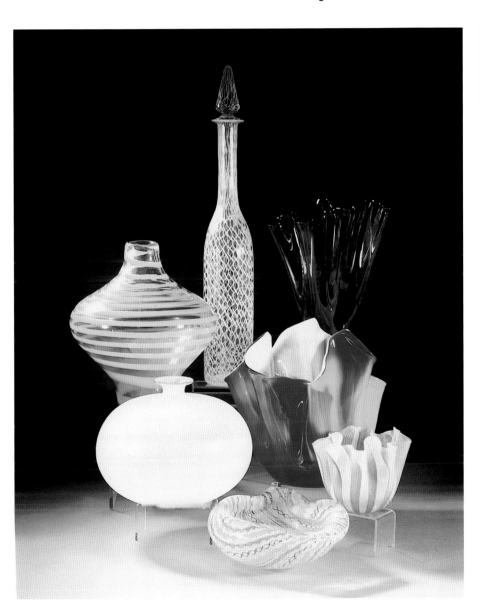

At a Glance

Date: Mid 20th century
Origin: Italy
Brief description: A group of decorative glassware produced by Venini at Murano, including two bulbous or globular vases, a tall and very slim decanter (back) and glasses or bowls in glass of different colors, textures, and treatments.

This group exhibits the versatility of this Venetian glassworks, which has long been renowned for its decorative wares. The company was founded by Paolo Venini (1895–1959) of Milan in 1921, in partnership with Giovanni Cappellin who took over the glassworks of the late Andrea Rioda and continued a tradition which had been in existence at Murano since the 16th century, though moving with the times and combining classical and modern styles with considerable flair.

Venini Glassware
mid 20th century

At a Glance

Date: Mid 20th Century
Origin: Italy
Brief description: A group of "A Canne" glassware by Venini, consisting of a water jug, vases, and a tall, slender decanter (center) composed of striped canes of various dark colors, contrasting with clear glass handles or stopper.

The original Venini company was dissolved in 1926 but Paolo Venini then reformed it to concentrate on mille-fiori glassware as well as developing many new surface treatments and color combinations. Venini not only designed glassware himself but recruited some of the most talented designers from other parts of Europe, with the result that his glassware, especially in the postwar period, was much more international in flavor, incorporating elements of Scandinavian and Spanish styles.

Murano Horse
mid 20th century

Murano is actually a small island near Venice where glassworkers have congregated since the 11th century. In 1292 the manufacture of glass in Venice itself was banned because of the fire hazard, and thereafter the industry was confined to Murano.

Today a visit to one or other of the glassworks of Murano is a major tourist attraction where visitors can see glass blown and intricate toys modeled in glass of many colors. Ornamental figures of animals such as this were aimed at the passing tourist trade but have become eminently collectable.

Murano Glassware
late 20th century

At a Glance

Date: Late 20th century
Origin: Italy
Brief description: A selection
of Murano glassware.

This selection includes two pairs of figures modeled in glass canes of various colors, both clear and opaque, to produce quite startling effects. As well as bowls, vases, and boxes in glass of different colors and textures the glassworks of Murano are renowned for their figures of animals and birds, such as this realistic decoy duck (lower right). The piece (lower left) is a conceptional sculpture by Livio Seguso produced about 1970.

Viennese Crystal Tray
c.1880

At a Glance

Date: c.1880
Origin: Austria
Brief description: A Viennese silver-gilt, gem-set enamel, and rock crystal tray, attributed to Josef von Storck.

The shaped oval outline is set with engraved crystal medallions flanked by female caryatids and masks, while the central panel depicts the Chateau de Chenonceau. The handles at the sides are scroll shaped in the form of dragons, and the tray is set on an octagonal foot. In the second half of the 19th century Vienna produced a great amount of decorative enamelware ranging from snuff-boxes and other small objects of vertu to large pieces of furniture. Decorative crystal wares of this kind are believed to have been sub-contracted to J. & L. Lobmeyr, the well-known glassworks. Josef von Storck (1830–1902) was an architect and interior designer who specialized in the revival of Renaissance motifs.

Bohemian Vase and Bowl
c.1860

At a Glance

Date: c.1860
Origin: Bohemia
Brief description: Two examples of Bohemian glass using a combination of colored glass and white overlays.

On the left is a center bowl with a gilt-line ogee crenelated rim above a band of oval panels, one of which bears a bust portrait of a woman while the others reproduce bouquets of flowers. It is set on a knopped stem on a tall domed foot. The vase on the right combines a rich ruby glass with white overlay in a delicate arabesque motif, with contrasting bands around the neck and foot.

Bohemian Glassware
mid 19th century

This selection shows the range of different forms and treatments for which this region was renowned. The covered vase and goblet at both ends of the top row are in clear glass and are engraved in the Lobmeyr style. They flank three fine specimens of gilded enameled glassware which typified the Biedermeier period in the mid 19th century. The lower row shows a number of goblets and beakers in the celebrated Bohemian cranberry glass with Milchglas (milk glass) overlays, enameled with flowers and gilded on the rims.

Bohemian Glassware
19th century

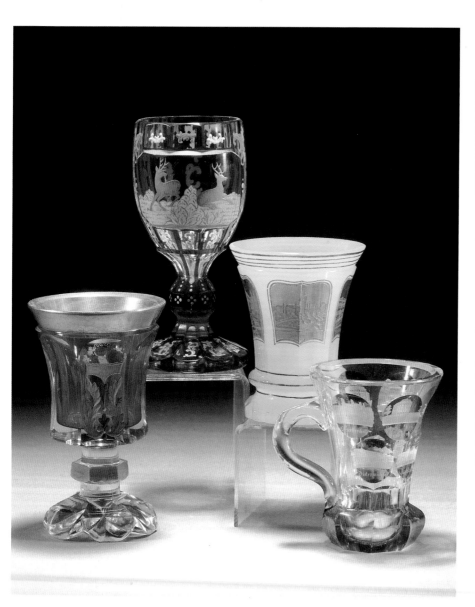

At a Glance

Date: 19th century
Origin: Bohemia
Brief description: A group
of Bohemian glassware
including a vase, enameled
cup, and goblets.

The group includes a fine vase in pale blue glass decorated with engraving and gilt panels and a handled cup ornamented with enamels and gilding applied to carved and engraved panels. On the left is a ruby flash cut and enameled goblet, cut with a rectangular panel showing an enameled scene of two stags, while the flutes are decorated with scrolls. The other fluted goblet is enameled, silvered and gilt with bowls of fruit above leaves on a knopped stem and petal cut foot.

Bohemian Glassware
late 19th century

At a Glance

Date: Late 19th century
Origin: Bohemia
Brief description: A group of Bohemian glassware including goblets, vases, and a floral centerpiece, wholly or partly of ruby or amethyst glass.

Though sometimes described loosely as cranberry glass (a term more applicable to the wares of Stourbridge and certain American glassworks) the Bohemian version is distinguished by its use of flashing, the imposition of a thin layer of glass of a contrasting color on to the original glass body. The colored overlay is then ground or engraved to reveal the underlying color. This technique was devized by the Romans and is to be found in medieval stained-glass windows, but it was revived in Bohemia in the Biedermeier period, and from there spread to England, America, and France.

Bohemian Goblet and Covered Glass
1870s

At a Glance

Date: 1870s
Origin: Bohemia
Brief description: A goblet and tall covered glass produced by the glassworks of Bohemia, showing fine examples of ruby flashed glass.

The flared bowl of the goblet has a continuous band of deer in a forest landscape, while the covered glass is carved and engraved. The enamels and gilding set off the ruby-flashed panels emulating classical cameos.

Loetz Glass Vase
c.1900

A glassworks was established at Klostermühle in Bohemia in 1830 by Johann Loetz. After his death in 1848 the company was run by his widow, hence the name of J. Loetz Witwe by which it is often known. Johann's grandson, Max Ritter von Spaun took over control of the factory in 1879 and, within a few years, had raised the company to a position of pre-eminence in Austrian glass. In the 1880s Loetz specialized in glass imitating semi-precious stones such as agate and aventurine. A decade later Loetz began producing iridescent glazes, improving upon the glazes pioneered by Tiffany in America.

Seguso Vase
c.1948

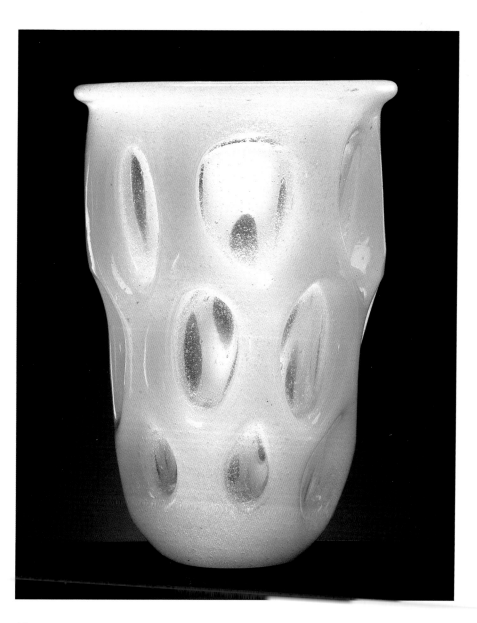

At a Glance

Date: c.1948
Origin: Italy
Brief description: An experimental "pulegoso" vase with clear glass "windows."

There is only one other similar example of this model known to exist and it is in the Archimede Seguso Collection, Murano, Italy.

Intarsia Bowl
1961

At a Glance

Date: 1961
Origin: Italy
Brief description: An Intarsia
bowl by Ercole Barovier
designed for Barovier & Toso.

The bowl has a very striking appearance due to the fused blue and amber
triangular panels. Benvenuto's son Ercole (1889–1974) formed Barovier & Toso
in 1936 as an amalgamation of two of Murano's oldest families and joining
forces with the brothers Artemio and Decio Toso. The company specialized in
large chandeliers and other lighting fixtures, but also produces decorative
pieces in a highly individual style. Intarsia glass was developed originally by
Frederick Carder at the Steuben Glass Works in America and in turn is derived
from the Italian term for inlaid woodwork.

Désiré Christian Vase
c.1900

At a Glance

Date: c.1900
Origin: France
Brief description: A vase
of swollen cylindrical shape
narrowing to a knopped neck,
decorated by Désiré Christian
whose engraved monogram
D. Ch. appears on the base.

*The clear glass is cased with col-
ored layers incorporating swirls
of varying shades of pink and
brown worked to reveal small
patches of green and white, and
is finely carved with flowers
and leaves.*

Bohemian Goblet
1909–1916

At a Glance

Date: 1909–1916
Origin: Bohemia
Brief description: A flashed glass goblet.

The goblet shows how far the traditional flashed glass had developed in the hands of one of the leading figures of the Sezession movement, Otto Prutscher (1880–1949). A professor at the Vienna Kunstgewerbeschule (school of decorative arts), Prutscher joined forces with his fellow professor Koloman Moser in 1903 to found the Wiener Werkstätte (Vienna workshops). Prutscher designed Art Nouveau glass for the Lötz glassworks, but then went on to produce a more restrained and angular style, such as this goblet, for Meyr's Neffe in the period leading up to World War I.

Centerpiece Coupe
late 19th century

The oval dish is cut with gadrooned and fluted ornaments, while the supporting frame is cast with rocaille ornament. The gilding is in fact ormolu, an alloy of copper, zinc, and tin which has the appearance of bright gold and was extensively used for the decoration of objects of all kinds and sizes, from snuff-boxes to picture frames and furniture. Mounts for glassware were very fashionable in France during the Second Empire and were made of bronze gilded by the mercuric process.

French Decorative Glassware
mid 19th century

At a Glance

Date: Mid 19th century
Origin: France
Brief description: A group of French decorative glassware mainly produced at the Clichy Glassworks.

This renowned factory was established by M. Rouyer and G. Maes at Billancourt in 1837 and moved to Clichy on the outskirts of Paris a few years later.

Although best-known for its millefiori paperweights, produced between 1846 and 1857, it also turned out a wide range of decorative glass, such as vases in colored glass with enameled decoration, goblets and wine-jugs in clear glass decorated with ruby or cranberry glass.

At the foot of the picture is a latticinio basket decorated with alternate stripes of green and white spiral threads, which is a variation on the fine colored glass canes that are used to make up the millefiori grounds of paperweights.

Daum Vases
c.1900

Jean Daum (1825–85) had operated a glassworks in Alsace but migrated to Nancy following the Franco-German War of 1870–71, where his native province was ceded to Germany, and established a glassworks there in 1875. After his death, the business was continued by his two sons Jean-Louis Auguste (1853–1909) and Jean-Antonin (1864–1930) who traded as Daum Brothers. They specialized in colored glass of this type, etched by hydrofluoric acid to create a sculptural effect.

Daum Vase
c.1900

At a Glance

Date: c.1900
Origin: France
Brief description:
An enameled vase by Daum.

The tapering cylindrical form swells towards the base over a circular foot. The textured surface is acid-etched and enameled in gilt, red and green with red flowerheads on spiked foliate stems. This type of tall, slender vase was a speciality of Daum and marketed by the firm under the name of Berluze.

Daum Box
early 20th century

At a Glance

Date: Early 20th century
Origin: France
Brief description: A Daum cameo glass box and cover.

The Daum factory produced ornamental boxes, bowls, and vases in this style, employing such combinations as opaque white over colored glass in which the outer layer was carved or wheel-engraved in order to reveal a pattern or motif in relief on the colored ground. In some cases, as in this box, glass of contrasting colors has the dark brown top layer cut away to reveal the yellow-brown underlay.

Daum Coupe
c.1900

At a Glance

Date: c.1900
Origin: France
Brief description: A Daum cameo and enameled glass coupe of irregular shape.

In this example, the blue overlay has been cut away to reveal an opaque ground, and the floral pattern has been enhanced by the use of enamels.

Daum Box
early 20th century

At a Glance

Date: Early 20th century
Origin: France
Brief description: A Daum cameo, enameled and gilt-edged glass box with matching cover, produced in the period immediately after World War I.

Paul (1890–1944) and Henri (1894–1966), the sons of Auguste, developed new styles and forms in the early 1920s as the more geometric patterns that typified the Art Deco period came into vogue.

Daum Bowl
c.1900

At a Glance

Date: c.1900
Origin: France
Brief description: A Daum bowl in clear green glass, acid-etched on the outer surface with a geometric design.

Michel Daum (born in 1900), the son of Antonin, seems to have been chiefly responsible for the diversification into clear glass objects, at first following traditional forms but later expanding into more sculptural pieces.

Argy-Rousseau Bowls and Vases
c.1920

At a Glance

Date: 1920
Origin: France
Brief description: A group of vases and bowls with *pâte-de-verre* decoration by Gabriel Argy-Rousseau (1885–1953).

This French craftsman developed this form of decoration using opaque glass of many colors applied and molded to a glass body of a contrasting color. Stylized flowers, berries, and branches were the most popular forms, but small animals were sometimes featured and are now much sought after.

Lalique Vase
c.1895

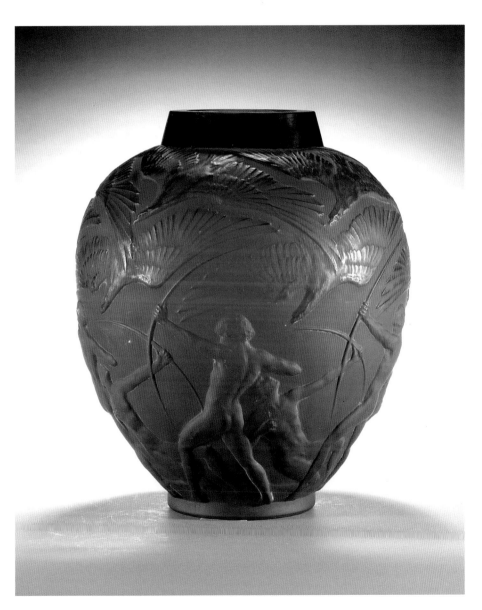

At a Glance

Date: c.1895
Origin: France
Brief description: A Lalique vase in amber glass, intaglio-molded with bas-reliefs of archers.

About 1895 Lalique began experimenting with molded glass, modeling his creations in wax. Plaster molds were then formed around the wax which was melted out and the molten glass run in. As the mold was destroyed, each piece of glass was unique. Very few of these experimental pieces appear to have survived intact.

Lalique Bowl
early 20th century

At a Glance

Date: Early 20th century
Origin: France
Brief description: A clear and
frosted glass bowl, wheel-
engraved by Lalique with the
descriptive title "Lys" and
model number 382 engraved
on the base.

*Like Gallé, Lalique was immense-
ly proud of his creations and in
the early period carefully
marked each piece. His glass
between 1909 and 1914 was
strongly influenced by the sinuous lines and ethereal qualities
of Art Nouveau and ranks with
the better-known products of
Gallé and Daum in the realms of
French art glass.*

Lalique Box
early 20th century

At a Glance

Date: Early 20th century
Origin: France
Brief description: A clear and opalescent box cover, the cardboard box base covered in silk with a R. Lalique mark

Lalique was a brilliant innovator, not only in the materials he used but also in the techniques he applied to them. These qualities are seen at their best in decorative pieces such as the series entitled *Deux Sirènes*. The glass box has a circular cover in a combination of clear and opalescent glass on which the figures of the two sirens are etched in such a manner as to suggest their ethereal quality.

Lalique Bowl
early 20th century

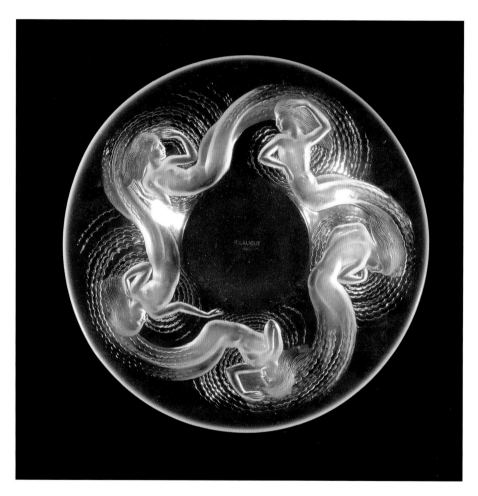

"Calypso" was the name given by Lalique to this bowl in a combination of clear, frosted and opalescent glass, perhaps an extension of the concept conveyed in the previous design, and inspired by the island nymph in Homer's Odyssey. In fact the bowl is decorated with five sinuous figures that writhe and gyrate around the circle. It is significant that Lalique, originally a jeweler, made his debut at the Salon in 1895, winning a third prize with a brooch depicting a female nude, the first time that he had turned to this subject.

Lalique Clock
1930

At a Glance

Date: 1930
Origin: France
Brief description: A clear and frosted table clock by Lalique.

Lalique also applied his carved and frosted glass technique to the ornamentation of clocks. "Deux Figurines" was the title given to this clear and frosted-glass table clock, on a gilt-metal base dated 1930. The two female figures are tastefully draped in gilt to suggest diaphanous robes, a prime example of the erotic element which Lalique brought to the decorative arts in the period between World War I and II.

Cros Mask
c.1890

Henri Cros (1840–1907) was a prominent French sculptor, who with his son Jean revived the technique of making various decorative objects, notably large panels in bas-relief, using pâte de verre. Cros studied modeling for several years at the Sèvres porcelain factory before adapting these techniques to glass. Pâte de verre (literally "glass paste") was produced by grinding glass to a powder, adding a fluxing medium and then coloring it with various oxides. The mixture was poured into a mold and fused at a high temperature. By the careful insertion of pieces of colored glass in the mold it was possible to create the effect of being studded with precious stones. This process, or something akin to it, had been used in ancient Egypt but it remained dormant for many centuries until Cros revived it. This particular mask was purchased in 1913 from Jean Cros by Louis Meley in whose family it remained until sold at Christie's in October 1998.

Decorchemont Glassware
c.1910–12

*Cros inspired other French artist-craftsmen who eventually surpassed him in their
use of* pâte de verre. *One of these was François-Emile Decorchemont (1880–1971)
who had previously worked as a ceramicist and painter at Conches, but who
established his own studio glassworks there in 1902. His early work consisted
mainly of figurines and small enameled bowls, but by 1905 he was evolving a
style using a roughened surface decorated with flowers and insects in low relief.
The selection was made between 1910 and 1945. After World War II he resumed
production, concentrating on opaque and marbled glass.*

Argy-Rousseau Bowl
c.1922

At a Glance

Date: c.1922
Origin: France
Brief description: A pâte de verre bowl entitled Aigles (eagles) by Gabriel Argy-Rousseau.

Argy-Rousseau (1885–1953) took this material a stage farther and evolved pâte de cristal which was much more transparent and has a very distinctive ring to it. It is employed in this instance, with a band of floral decoration round the rim interspersed with figures of eagles in flight. Argy-Rousseau also made lamps, plafonniers (ceiling lights), and figurines in this material.

Vides Poches
early 20th century

At a Glance

Date: Early 20th century
Origin: France
Brief description: A group of small *pâte de verre* articles known as vides poches.

These vides poches *(literally "empty pockets") were created by the sculptor Henri Bergé for Amalric Walter (1870–1959), an artist and glassworker of the Nancy School who was active at the turn of the 20th century. From 1906 till the outbreak of World War I, Walter had a contract with Daum whereby he was allowed to use their plant and machinery in the production of his decorative wares, but after the war he established his own factory where the production of art glass has continued to this day.*

Schneider Tazza
c.1925

This glassworks was founded in 1908 at Epinay-sur-Seine by Charles Schneider (1881–1962) who had previously trained as a glass decorator under Gallé and Daum. At first Schneider produced relatively plain glassware, but after World War I he branched out into decorative glass in the Art Nouveau tradition, often using subtle combinations of two or three colors, cased or flashed, and sometimes with acid-etched relief. Tazze of this type were a popular subject of this glasshouse.

Schneider Vase
c.1925

At a Glance

Date: c.1925
Origin: France
Brief description: A Schneider vase in dark red opalescent glass streaked with blue and black, with handles of pink and clear glass.

Pieces of the prewar period were simply signed "Schneider" as in this case, but in more recent years products were marked "Le Verre Française." Schneider's son Robert took over in 1948 and in 1962 moved the factory to Lorris (Loire).

Tiffany Lamps
early 20th century

At a Glance

Date: Early 20th century
Origin: United States
Brief description: A "turtle-back" desk lamp and a leaded glass and bronze "Poppy" table lamp, both from the Tiffany Studios, New York.

Louis Comfort Tiffany (1848–1933), the son of a celebrated goldsmith and jeweler, Charles Lewis Tiffany, studied art and established a firm of interior decorators which became one of the best-known firms in New York, a by-word for elegance and luxury. In 1892, he purchased a failing glassworks at Corona, New York, and opened his own factory the following year. Interestingly, the great bulk of the first year's production went straight into museums. By 1901, Tiffany had produced a wide variety of iridescent and opalescent glass. Leaded glass was another speciality, used to great effect in lampshades, paneling, and windows.

Tiffany Vase
early 20th century

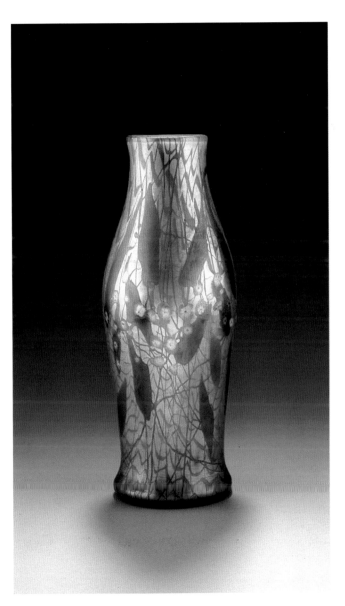

At a Glance

Date: Early 20th century
Origin: United States
Brief description: A millefiore favrile glass vase from the Tiffany Studios.

Arthur Nash (1849–1934), born at Stratford-upon-Avon and at one time a partner in the Whitehouse Glass Works in Stourbridge before emigrating to the United States in 1892, was involved in the establishment of the Corona glassworks and is usually regarded as the inventor of the distinctive "Favrile" glass for which Tiffany was renowned. Brilliant shades of greens, blues, yellows, and browns and motifs such as peacock's feathers, sea-weed, and ferns characterize Favrile ware.

This vase was presented as a gift to John Winter, who worked as a maitre d' at the restaurant Louis Sherry's in New York City, from Louis Comfort Tiffany, one of the restaurant's patrons. When John Winter died in 1925, the vase was given to his wife, who gave it to their granddaughter in 1959.

Tiffany Vase
c.1910

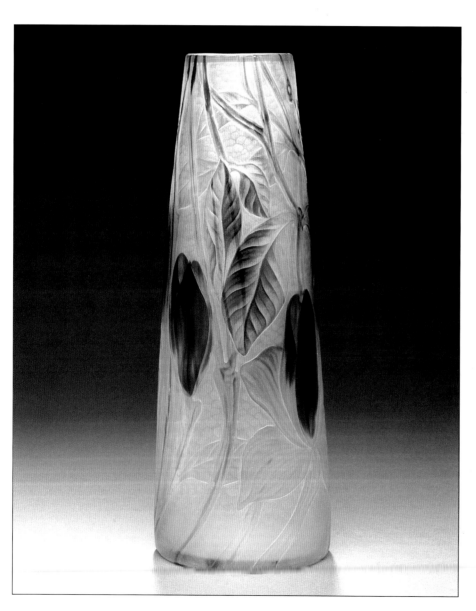

At a Glance

Date: c.1910
Origin: U.S.A.
Brief description: A wheel-carved cameo Favrile vase from Tiffany Studios.

The frosted ground is carved with purple magnolia blossoms and green leaves amid pendant vines. Favrile was also noted for its stunning effects, such as lava or bronze long buried in the soil, but the range was quite fantastic. By the end of the 19th century Tiffany was producing thousands of decorative glass articles each year and even got the contract to refurnish the White House.

Tiffany Lamp
c.1906

*Although the plant of this name
is spelled Wisteria, Tiffany
deliberately chose this form
after the botanist Caspar Wistar
(1761–1818) who had been
professor of anatomy at the
University of Pennsylvania soon
after its foundation. Naturalistic
glass lamps of this type were a
Tiffany speciality, a hangover
from Tiffany's earliest
experiments with stained-glass
windows. Lamps were also
produced in a multitude of
shades shaped like bell-flowers
or decorated with dragonflies.*

Steuben Bowl
c.1910

Date: c.1910
Origin: U.S.A.
Brief description: A pair of glass center bowls and a matching punch bowl by Steuben.

The Steuben Glass Company was formed at Corning, New York, in 1903 under the management of Thomas G. Hawkes and Frederick Carder (1863–1963), an English glass designer formerly employed at Stourbridge till 1903 when he emigrated to America with the express purpose of setting up on his own account. Subsequently he became one of the most prominent figures in the later history of American art glass. In 1918, the Steuben Company was taken over by the Corning Company but Carder continued to direct operations till the 1930s.

Clutha Bowl and Vase
c.1890

Couper operated a glassworks which had been founded at Bathgate, West Lothian in 1866 and continued until 1887 and subsequently moved to Glasgow. In the 1890s Couper commissioned Christopher Dresser (1834–1904) to design distinctive glass in the Art Nouveau idiom and Clutha (from the Gaelic name for the River Clyde) was evolved.

Leerdam Canister, Jug, and Dishes
1924

At a Glance

Date: 1924
Origin: Holland
Brief description: A yellow pressed-glass canister, jug, and stand and two hexagonal dishes designed by Hendrik Petrus Berlage and P. Zwart for Leerdam of Holland.

The canister in keeping with the rest of the service is of hexagonal form with raised hexagonal finial on a fitted hexagonal stand. These pieces are marked with the artist's monogram HPB and Ontbijtservies I ("breakfast service"). Berlage (1856–1934) was one of the most prominent Dutch architects and townplanners of the early 20th century and was greatly influenced by Frank Lloyd Wright. Although best remembered for the Amsterdam Bourse and Holland House in London, he also worked as an interior decorator and designed a wide range of furniture, ceramics, and glassware such as this.

Clichy, Baccarat, and St Louis Weights
mid 19th Century

At a Glance

Date: Mid 19th century
Origin: France
Brief description: A selection of Clichy, Baccarat, and St Louis glass paperweights.

A Clichy faceted millefiori mushroom weight (top left); a Clichy millefiori containing roses (top right); a St. Louis millefiori weight (middle left); a Clichy weight showing the profile of Queen Victoria (middle right); a St. Louis millefiori weight (bottom left); and (bottom right) a Baccarat "swan on a pond" weight, the hollow interior enclosing a white swan.

A glassworks was established in the village of St Louis, Lorraine, in 1767. By the 1830s, it was specializing in colored glassware and in 1832 it combined with Baccarat to purchase the Creusot glassworks. This established Baccarat and St Louis as the two leading glass manufacturers in France.

Pantin Weight
c.1878

At a Glance

Date: c.1878
Origin: France
Brief description: A magnum lizard glass paperweight.

Pantin's large lizard and salamander weights represent the acme of paperweights. In this weight the black reptile spotted with yellow crouches in an alert attitude between two flowering plants. A glassworks existed at Pantin from 1850 although it only came to be known by its present name in 1900. The zenith of its paperweight production was in the late 1870s when the company was known as Monot, Père et Fils et Stumpf which created a sensation wih its large weights at the Paris Exposition of 1878.

Clichy Weight
c.1878

At a Glance

Date: c.1878
Origin: France
Brief description: A large fruit weight with three pears and a peach in a latticinio basket from an unidentified French factory, possibly Clichy.

This very realistic weight has a large russet-brown pear, two smaller ripe pears, and a peach, each with a dark brown stalk, three of which are set with opposing green leaves, contained in a deep basket of loosely woven white latticinio thread, the rim of the basket edged with a turquoise ribbon. No other comparable weight appears to be recorded. Although the fruit does bear similarities to those found in St Louis weights, the fluorescence of this example is a slightly cloudy pale lime-green more consistent with that of the Clichy weights. A Clichy weight with a single large pear has been recorded so on balance it seems likely that this unique example came from that factory.

Clichy, Gillander & Sons, and Ysart Weights
mid 19th/20th century

A t   a   G l a n c e

Date: Mid 19th/20th century
Origin: France/ United States
Brief description:
A possible Gillinder & Sons weight, five Clichy weights, and a Paul Ysart weight.

A pink carpet-ground weight, c.1870, perhaps Gillander & Sons (top left); a Clichy swirl weight, mid 19th century (top right); a Paul Ysart garlanded sulphide weight, 20th century, depicting the head of a Muse (middle left); a Clichy red-ground, mille-fiori weight, mid 19th century; (middle right); a Clichy daisy weight, mid 19th century, (bottom left); and a Clichy initialled blue-ground millefiori weight, mid 19th century (bottom right).

Clichy, Baccarat, and St Louis Weights
19th century

A Clichy millefiori weight (top left); a St Louis crown weight (top right); a St Louis marbrie weight (middle left); a St Louis spaced concentric millefiori weight (middle right); a Clichy millefiori weight (bottom left); and (bottom right) a Baccarat millefiori weight.

The third of the great French glasshouses to specialize in paperweights was founded by Joseph Maes at Billancourt in 1837 and moved to Clichy-la-Garenne on the outskirts of Paris two years later. Initially Clichy concentrated on domestic wares for the lower end of the market, but by the early 1840s had begun to develop more expensive wares for export. As early as 1844, its decorative glass was drawing favorable comparisons with that of Baccarat and St Louis.

Clichy, Baccarat, and St Louis Weights
19th Century

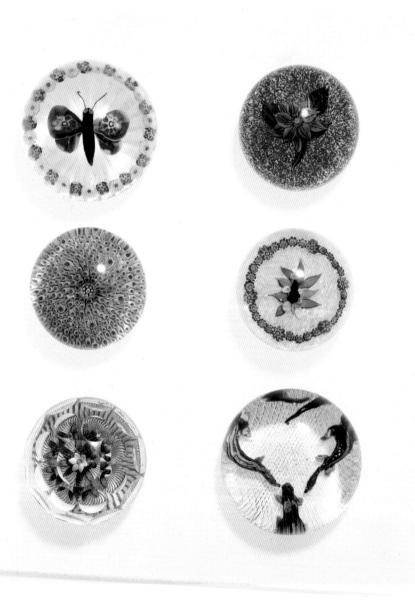

A Baccarat garlanded butterfly weight (top left); a St Louis jasper-ground yellow dahlia weight (top right); a St Louis pink carpet-ground weight (middle left); a Clichy garlanded fruit and posy weight(middle right); a St Louis faceted upright bouquet weight (bottom left); and (bottom right) a St Louis salamander and frog weight.

When St Louis dropped out of paperweight production about 1850 Clichy stepped in and filled the orders with which their competitors were unable or unwilling to deal. Clichy was the sole French firm to participate in the glass section at the Great Exhibition of 1862 in London and continued to make fine paperweights until the end of that decade.

Baccarat and St Louis Weights
mid 19th century

At a Glance

Date: Mid 19th century
Origin: France
Brief description:
Three St Louis and two
Baccarat glass paperweights.

A St Louis pear weight (top right); a Baccarat pear weight (top left); a St Louis pear weight (middle right); a St Louis apple weight (bottom left); and a Baccarat pear weight (bottom right).

Clichy, Baccarat, and St Louis Weights
mid 19th century

A Baccarat garlanded blue and white buttercup weight (top left); a St Louis purple dahlia weight (top right); a Clichy blue-ground flower weight (center); a Baccarat faceted upright bouquet weight (bottom left); and (bottom right) a St Louis faceted upright bouquet weight.

Baccarat and St Louis Weights
mid 19th century

At a Glance

Date: Mid 19th century
Origin: France
Brief description: Four St Louis and two Baccarat weights.

Two St Louis crown weights with entwined latticinio threads (top row); two large St Louis faceted cherry weights (middle row); a Baccarat faceted double-overlay concentric millefiori mushroom (bottom left); and (bottom right) a Baccarat faceted flat bouquet weight.

A Baccarat Weight
mid 19th century

Six white buds grow from either side of conjoined green stalks with numerous green leaves on a star-cut base.

A Baccarat Mushroom Weight
mid 19th century

The tuft is composed of tightly packed multi-colored millefiori canes, set within a torsade of white cable with a cobalt-blue ribbon. The glassworks in the Alsatian town of Baccarat could trace its origins back to 1764 although it did not acquire its present name until 1822. It displayed paperweights at the Paris exhibitions of 1844 and 1849 but no weights were exhibited in 1855 or 1878, so it must be assumed that paperweight production had generally ceased by about 1850, although a few isolated examples with dated canes have been recorded up to 1858. Interestingly, production of paperweights was revived a century later and continues to this day.

Ysart Butterfly Weight
c.1930

At a Glance

Date: c.1930
Origin: Scotland
Brief description: A butterfly weight by Paul Ysart.

A magnum Paul Ysart butterfly weight. The insect has a purple and white body, pink antennae with orange tips, and wings composed of assorted canes in shades of yellow, green, grey, orange, and white, set on a translucent amethyst ground.

Paul Ysart was born in Barcelona in 1904 of Bohemian parentage, and settled in Scotland in 1915. He worked at the Leith Flint Glassworks before establishing his own business, specializing in the production of paperweights. Out of this developed several other businesses— Monart, Vasart, Strathearn, Perthshire Paperweights, and the paperweight division of Caithness Glass.

Bohemian Lusters
c.1860

At a Glance

Date: c.1860
Origin: Bohemia
Brief description: Two pairs of Bohemian white-overlay lusters.

The floriform bowls have gilt-line ogee rims above a band of raised ovals painted with portrait medallions of children and bouquets of flowers, suspended by prism drops, above clear stems and feet overlayed by a lappit border. The term luster was applied to either free-standing or hanging clusters of prismatic glass which were designed to catch the light from candles or oil lamps and reflect it for maximum brightness and decorative effect.

Table Lamps
late 19th century

At a Glance

Date: Late 19th century
Origin: Bohemia
Brief description: A pair of late-Victorian gilt-bronze mounted Bohemian glass table lamps.

The twin columns are of opaque Milchglas decorated with clear ruby glass and star-cut ornament. The spreading foliate cast bases and finials have gadrooned borders.

Cut-glass Candlesticks
19th century

In each case the baluster stem is deep-cut with circular incized feet, the facetting and icicle pendants designed to catch and reflect the light to maximum effect. Candelabra of this type were usually produced in pairs, intended to stand at either end of a side-table and placed in front of a mirror reflect the brilliance of the glass. Early examples were relatively plain, but by the beginning of the 19th century they were often extravagantly festooned with drops, icicles, and prismatic rods.

Ormolu and Cut-glass Chandelier
18th/19th Century

At a Glance

Date: c. end of 18th or beginning of the 19th century
Origin: Russia
Brief description: A Russian ormolu and cut-glass eight-branch chandelier.

From the corona hangs droplets and issuing beaded arches with further droplets, while the central shaft has large pendants. The eight branches are mounted above a tapering lower tier. The chandelier was developed at Venice early in the 18th century and rapidly became the principal lighting fixture designed to be suspended from the ceiling. Early forms had conspicuous metal frames but as the century wore on frames became lighter and much greater prominence was given to the glass. By the middle of the 18th century glass pendants and drops came into fashion and became increasingly profuse and elaborate right through the Victorian period.

Birdcage Lantern
early 20th century

*Supported by a ring handle,
the shaped cylindrical body has
domed upper and lower sec-
tions, covered all over with
acanthus leaves and pierced
scrolls, with a pine-cone lower
finial. Although the inner case is
of glass, in this instance it is of
secondary importance to the
metal mounting.*

Giltwood Mirror
18th century

This George III giltwood mirror has an oval plate and frame carved with foliage and flower-heads entwined with ribbons. The base has crossed branches and C-scrolls while the crest has an acanthus spray entwined with C-scrolls. The plate is of later date and the frame has been regilded.

Girandole
18th Century

At a Glance

Date: 18th century
Origin: England
Brief description:
One of a pair of George III
giltwood girandoles.

This giltwood girandole has an asymmetric divided plate, the deep frame carved with broad scolls of acanthus and gadrooning. The two scrolling foliate branches frame the figure of a Chinaman seated on rockwork and holding a lantern. The mirrored crest has an acanthus foliage canopy in the form of a pagoda.

Regency Mirrors
c.1810

At a Glance

Date: c.1810
Origin: England
Brief description: A pair of Regency giltwood and *verre églomisé* mirrors.

Each mirror has a rectangular plate between fluted, foliate headed pilasters, with an inverted breakfront and a ball-encrusted cornice. The panels at the top depict naval scenes. Verre églomisé *was a process of drawing and painting on the reverse side of a glass panel, then backing the decoration with metal foil, usually in gold or silver leaf. The term is derived from the Parisian artists and print-collector Jean-Baptiste Glomy who is credited with inventing an improved method of framing prints with black and gold fillets painted from behind the glass.*

Regency Mirror
c.1810

At a Glance

Date: c.1810
Origin: England
Brief description: A Regency *verre églomisé* giltwood and gesso pier mirror.

The ebonized frieze has ribbon-tied foliate ornament with a verre églomisé *frieze of gilt garlands with similar floral decoration on the twin side panels. Individual pictures in this technique are comparatively rare, but its use as ornament in the panels surrounding mirrors attained the height of popularity in the early 19th century. The same technique was widely used in the ornamentation of longcase clocks in the same period.*

Overmantel Mirror
19th century

At a Glance

Date: 19th century
Origin: England
Brief description: A large giltwood overmantel mirror.

The baluster columnar uprights are headed by ram's masks while the arched top is surmounted by an oval escutcheon tied by a ribbon and flanked by a pair of cherubs and scrolling foliage. The arched plate is contained within a beaded border and molded frame.

Giltwood Mirror
c.1925

At a Glance

Date: c.1925
Origin: Austria
Brief description: A giltwood mirror from the Wiener Werkstätte, decorated with an overlapping stylized leaf motif.

This giltwood mirror has a rectangular frame partially painted white, with gilt decoration and surmounted with similarly decorated carved openwork simulating branches of fruit and leaves. It still possesses its original Wiener Werkstätte label from the mid 1920s. It was designed by Dagobert Peche, one of the leading artist-craftsmen in Vienna in the 1920s, noted for his naturalistic treatment of silver, ceramics, glass, and furniture.

Hoffmann Vitrine
c.1905

At a Glance

Date: c.1905
Origin: Austria
Brief description: An
ebonized bent wood vitrine.

A vitrine such as this would have
been used to display art objects.
This piece dates from 1905 and
is attributed to Josef Hoffmann.
Josef Hoffmann (1870–1935)
studied under Otto Wagner at
the Vienna Academy where he
won the Rome Prize in 1895 and
subsequently studied architecture in Italy for a year before
returning to Vienna where he
worked with Joseph Maria
Olbrich in Wagner's drawing
office. At Olbrich's instigation he
joined the Association of
Austrian Visual Artists in 1897,
but resigned with several others
to form the Vienna Sezession.
Thereafter he took a leading
part in the arts and crafts movement in Austria. Throughout his
long and varied career he exer-
cised an enormous influence on
the development of the
applied arts in Europe.

Frank Lloyd Wright Leaded Windows
c.1911

At a Glance

Date: c.1911
Origin: U.S.A.
Brief description: A pair of leaded-glass windows designed by Frank Lloyd Wright (1869–1959) for the Lake Geneva Hotel, Lake Geneva, Wisconsin.

The rectilinear design has a chevron motif incorporating colors of amber, pale green, opalescent white, and purple. Frank Lloyd Wright was the most influential architect and interior designer of his era.

Index